Introduction
From
Stephen Lee Ostrowski

Before the invention of the internet, few of us were subjected to the plague of scams that have appeared with the aid of modern technology. In pre-internet days you may have been short changed on a botched building job, or were sold a faulty car which may have cost several hundred dollars to put right. You could even have been the recipient of a chain mail scam. None of this compares to the deluge of mind boggling junk thrown at us in this day and age. Today, internet users are bombarded with products they have no interest in. Even if they do succumb to an offer that seems like a bargain, they may get stung for additional services which they didn't want, on top of the initial payment for the item that they purchased. Always read the small print, and look out for hidden "membership fees". If you have been scammed in this manner it's likely that the first you'll know about it is when you scroll through your bank statement and start to question unfamiliar payments being withdrawn from your bank account. These are often referred as "Hidden payment scams". But these are only the tip of the iceberg. Online scams come in a multitude of various disguises and we'll look at some of the most common ones.

Inheritance Scams

In this form of scam the recipient receives an e-mail from a "lawyer" informing them that a wealthy businessman, tycoon, or a member of a Royal family, such as a Prince, has passed away, and you have inherited a small fortune. This notification from the bogus lawyer claims that he/she is acting on behalf of the deceased. Because the dead person concerned has no immediate family, the lawyer has found information that leads him to believe that you are the beneficiary of the last will and testament left by the deceased, because you have some historic bloodline in relation to the deceased, or you may simply have the same surname as the deceased. You may be forgiven for thinking that all your Christmases have come together at once upon reading such an e-mail. If you fall for this story of extraordinary generosity from a complete stranger, then you might wise up at the next stage of this sting. Initially, you may have been offered an inheritance of several million dollars from the friendly seemingly helpful lawyer, but to obtain this huge windfall there are several up-front fees to pay which will include a release fee, legal documentation fees, lawyer's fees etc etc, which may add up to a few thousand dollars. You will be asked to send these payments to a contact via Western Union or Moneygram in exchange for a "Certificate of Entitlement" to your impending fortune. This of course, isn't worth a peanut, and once you have sent your payment to these crooks, it can rarely or never be recovered. These kinds of scams are loosely categorised under the code 419, which is the Nigerian criminal code for Internet "Advance Fee" fraud scams. If you have been unlucky enough to fall for this type of scam you could be just as easily fooled by the "Recovery scam" in which an associate of the scammer that you lost your money to, will claim that he will be able to recover your money, but for a fee of course….so the whole cycle starts over again and you find yourself being ripped off twice in succession. Nearly all these scams originate from West African countries, Nigeria being the most common. Ghana is also a scam hot spot, as is South Africa, and Malaysia in South East Asia.

Romance Scams

In chat rooms, forums, dating sites, and social media sites such as Facebook and Twitter to name but a few, you can easily create an avatar profile or invent your alter-ego without ever having to reveal your true identity. Most users however, are looking for honest interaction with their fellow internet surfers while making new friends and contacts along the way…. or may even be looking for love. But there are pitfalls. Inexperienced internet users or relative newcomers to this global melting pot of social activity can find the internet somewhat confusing and are unaware of the dangers that lurk. Everything is not quite what it seems. Many dating sites are full of scammers, as are the most popular social media sites, such as Facebook, which is by far the most widely used. Facebook currently has over 1.5 billion users. It is estimated that as many as 170 million of user profiles are fakes, and do not reflect the users true identity. There may be legitimate reasons in some cases where the user may be simply trying to protect their true identity, or may be using the service as a simple means of escapism, voyeurism, or to indulge in hotly debated topics without any fear of reprisals. But…. the World Wide Web has become a bubbling cauldron of deceit and criminality where the innocent can be easily deceived.

Romance scams take several forms of approach, either through unsolicited e-mails, or through many different social media sites like Facebook, Badoo, and Instagram etc. The list is endless. Both men and women are targets of the romance scammer. Typically, the romance scammer will target victims in the 40 – 60 age bracket, although not necessarily in every case. This does however seem to be the scammer's chosen preference. The reason for this is that many people in this age group have reached a point in life where they may have lost a partner through ill health and after a period of grieving, they feel the need to meet somebody to fill the void in their life. The same can be said of divorcees, lifelong singles, and those with marriage problems. Indeed, many of the people who fall in to these categories are often going through a mid-life crisis and look to internet dating to rebuild their self esteem and their confidence. With carefully chosen words, and pre-scripted romantic drivel, together with glamorous stolen photos, the romance scammers will say all the things that a lonely heart wants to hear… and more.

Men are commonly targeted by romance scammers from Eastern European countries, notably Russia and Ukraine. The victim may be drawn away from the dating site where the initial introduction took place, and invited to participate in a private exchange of e-mails. From this point on the victim is presented with a pre-written script all about Anastasia, Natalya, or whatever her name is explaining that she is desperately unhappy in her native Russia and is looking for love beyond the borders of the post communist soviet block. Stunning photos will accompany each e-mail in an effort to snare their victim. The purpose of all this is to obtain money through deception. They aim to coax the victim into sending them money to finance the purchase of a plane ticket and a visa which would allow them to fly to your home town with the promise that the relationship will be consummated and the union will lead to eternal happiness. The reality is that once you have sent the money they have requested through the usual channels (Western Union or Moneygram) you will never hear from the love of your life again. Contact will be broken and you could end up several hundreds or thousands of dollars out of pocket.

This tried and trusted method of deception is similar in context to the approach used by African scammers who target women. One of the most successful platforms in the scammers search for love hungry middle-aged women is Facebook.

On-line scamming in Nigeria creates a large slice of the country's wealth and economy. It is by far one of the most corrupt nations on Earth. Neighbouring countries such as Ghana are not that far behind. Women, by nature, are usually far more susceptible to romance scams, thus allowing seasoned scammers to accumulate more wealth than they could have imagined before the conception of on-line social media. The most commonly used tactic by the African scammer is to create a false profile using the stolen photos of currently serving, or deceased U.S military personnel, claiming to be on deployment in Syria, Iraq, or Afghanistan. The picture they will try to paint is of a lonely soldier of good standing who is a proud and "God fearing man" (a term often used) who lost his wife under tragic circumstances, either through cancer, or an automobile accident. Consequently, this will have left him widowed with one or more young children to take care of who are usually in a boarding school somewhere. The scammer and his associates will sift through hundreds and thousands of profiles of middle-aged women who they perceive to be easy targets, and then introduce themselves in the following manner once you have accepted their friend request. A typical opening line of introduction is as follows: "Hello my dear… I look your profile and see that you are beautiful. I look for good woman for lasting relationship and good mother for my son. I live United state but with peace keeping mission in Afghanistan and like to know you better. Hope you having a good day". The very poor grammar should tell you straight away that he is not from the United States, or anywhere for that matter outside of Africa. Another giveaway is that almost by default, the scammers will give themselves names comprising of two Christian names, or back to front Christian names and surnames such as "Johnston Fred", "Peters David", "Frank John", "Daniel Stephen"… and so on. There are thousands of possible poor combinations such as these. If the victim fails to notice these red flags then within weeks of exchanging messages, the romance scammer will soon declare his undying love for his victim, followed by tales of his unfortunate financial standing. A number of possible scenarios will follow:

1. He cannot use his Visa card as there are no working or accessible ATM machines in his vicinity (being a war zone and all that)
2. He has no access to his salary and cannot afford to eat (The military feed their troops well)
3. His son/daughter is sick in some medical facility or hospital in some other country and he needs to send money there to pay for medical bills (You may have already been sent a photo of his angelic looking child so this ruse might tug at your heartstrings)
4. He wants to come and visit you, but there is a fee to pay to the military vacation department to allow him to do so. But of course….

he can't pay the fee as he has no access to his money. (Military leave is non-negotiable and it doesn't have to be paid for)

5. His service time has ended and he wants you to send him enough money to purchase an airline ticket so that he can fly directly to you and fulfil his promises of love and marriage. (Army personnel are taken to and from deployment zones in military transport carriers. They don't use civilian aircraft)

In fact, there are a number of similar sob stories that are crafted to appeal to the soft side of the victim's nature. In each case the victim will be asked for financial assistance to be sent via Western Union or Moneygram and often unsurprisingly, to a recipient based in Nigeria, or Ghana. If all those warning flags pass you by and you start to send money, then you are on the slippery slope to financial ruin. Once the scammer has captured your heart, you will be like putty in their grubby hands, and the requests for money will keep coming. You will feel compelled to continue sending money in the vague hope that the relationship will come good and there will be a "happy ever after" outcome. It won't happen. Too often the victim is left broke and destitute before they even begin to realize that they have been scammed.

In previous books I have published I have assumed the role of scam-baiter. In my three books entitled: "Hello My New Best Friend" "Gerty Bites Back" and "Gerty Bites Again" I ridicule and humiliate scammers into submission, best described by one reader as a "Hilarious crusade of revenge". However, I have only ever touched lightly on the serious nature of romance scams and the devastating effect such scams inflict upon the victims. Ordinary people looking for love and companionship are cruelly taken advantage of by these heartless parasites whose sole aim is to relieve them of their life savings.

Ever since I took an interest some years back in romance scams, I have been in contact with many such victims and have read the heartbreaking accounts of their collective experiences. This is of course, from those who choose to discuss the subject. There are many victims who won't talk about their experience at the hands of scammers, and have become emotionally withdrawn and unable to come to terms with their financial losses and the heartache that comes hand in hand with being a victim of a romance scam. In worst case scenarios it can lead to thoughts of suicide, and tragically, even suicide itself....

Foreword
From
Judi Huggins

Back in November 2014, it had been almost a year since I had spoken to my friend Jane. During our last conversation Jane had told me that she had found love with a man she had met on Facebook, with whom she had been exchanging messages with for some time. She was full of enthusiasm and looking back, the early signs of obsession were obvious. It was always in the back of my mind however, and I often wondered how this relationship might have developed as I'd heard nothing from her in the year that had passed. We had always been close and both of us seemed to know when something was wrong, or if one of us was ill for example, but in recent years we had both been pre-occupied with our own lives, work, and families, or so I assumed in Jane's case. Well… today I decided it was time to phone Jane. I phoned her several times and got no answer and no return call.

It took me 15 minutes to walk over to Jane's house. On an average day, it would have taken me 25 minutes. I guess I was just eager to see her. She certainly wouldn't have moved without telling me. I rang the doorbell for some time. If I didn't get an answer soon, I would try again tomorrow….and the day after that.

Jane finally opened the front door, looking thin and dishevelled, with a gaunt look on her face, which was so unlike the Jane I knew. I asked if she felt alright. Did something happen that made her as unhappy as she looked? She mumbled something about "Dean Simon" and reached over to her desk and picked up a stack of folders and papers. She asked me to keep them at my house for a while and to read them all in my own time. She said she had something that she wanted me to do, and when the time was right, she would explain further. I simply did as she asked, quietly closed her front door, and took the stack of papers home with me.

The following day I began reading all the papers which consisted of social media chats, phone conversations, money transfers, and photos of a father and son who all these papers related to. It made for uncomfortable reading and a sinister story was beginning to unfold. Jane and I had been friends as far back as I can remember, but nonetheless, this was not what I expected. I felt that she may have been sharing too much personal information with me, and that it might be difficult to take on board. It took several days to read the dozens of letters that Jane and her online lover had written to each other. After reading all of this correspondence I pieced together what had been going on in her life during the time I hadn't seen her. Then I got a feeling of all the torment she had been living through and why she looked the way she did. She had clearly been the victim of an elaborate romance scam, which had cost her dearly.

Having no wish to see Jane suffer in silence I opted to stay with her for a few days to be certain she wasn't sinking deeper into depression, and that she was at least taking care of her basic needs. The days I spent with Jane were difficult. She barely ate and she tried to convince me to leave so she could take an overdose to end the misery and despair she was going through. I needed to take control of this situation. Even her immediate family it seems were unaware of the extent of her depression.

I wrote down a list of things that I thought Jane could accomplish, which would help alleviate the obvious misery and torment she was experiencing. We would attempt to get her life back. She would have to fight to live. My goal was to try to help her to put this experience behind her. We removed everything negative in her house, whether it was poetry, photos, her late husband's unnecessary clothing, or items on her phone and her computer that represented her time with her scammer. Past memories were staring her in the face night and day. We had to start a healing process.

With some trepidation, Jane asked me to write her story, but I needed a better feel of what she was dealing with emotionally. It was then that I decided to find out for myself how she was drawn into this scam. I became a potential victim myself. I joined several dating and social media sites in the hope that I would run into Jane's online lover. Part of me wanted him caught and punished, the other part of me wanted to make him suffer in unthinkable ways. I held on to a selection of the men I met online in an effort to snare myself a scammer, and with any luck, to hopefully find Jane's scammer. I chose the smart clever ones who sweet-talked their victims and claimed to have lucrative careers in the armed forces or construction. I wanted all the attention they could give me and I wanted to face the same challenges my friend had endured for the past two years or so. I added drama into my stories. If I couldn't provide a convincing story in the beginning of our meeting, then I would create an accident later. I would usually have some story from the start just to fit it into a tragedy at the end. I had to have an escape route. At first I used my true identity and photo because I kind of jumped into the venture with little or no thought as to the possible consequences. I threw caution to the wind and dared them to threaten me in some way. More often than not, the dubious characters I met would ask for money within a week. The really clever ones would make sure they had hooked their victim who was keen from the start, and if it took months trying to break me down with romantic poetry and promises of love and marriage, they still held on as I gave the impression that I was very wealthy, because money is the scammer's sole objective. No matter what the outcome, I started to turn in, and report, an average of 30 to 35 scammers a month. I had them removed from various sites after their repeated requests for money. I actually started enjoying the game as I felt nothing but contempt for their approach to vulnerable women who are simply looking for companionship or a genuine long term partner. In time, I had a clear understanding of the victim's roll in a scam and how the scammer can win your heart, and then leave it shattered. I learned to allow them to be my "best friend," one so charming and so eager to please. The scammers are taught to say the right things to suit the moment. They can cry at the drop of a pin. Jane had said of her scammer: "If he's been lying, then he is an Academy Award winner, because he had me so convinced, and I am never easily fooled"

I joined support groups on Facebook that catered for scam victims, as did Jane eventually, and I spent time reading about other people's similar experiences. I singled out one particular group that seemed to be the most informative and user friendly. That was when I met Stephen Lee Ostrowski who was one of the founder members and one of three group administrators. Stephen had been baiting romance scammers for years in his own unique way and his posts to the group are an integral part of the content, and they brought humor to an otherwise sad exchange of stories from the hundreds of members who posted their thoughts and personal experiences week in week out. Stephen said to me: "If you can laugh in the face of adversity then you have started the healing process"…. and his baiting exploits are genuinely funny. I had been with the group for over a year and a half while learning from the best. I had the privilege of reading Stephen's books, and in passing conversation I asked him if he had ever thought about writing a true story about a real life scam victim. He said he had hoped to do just that, but felt that chance may pass him by because people were often afraid to reveal the exact details of how they were scammed and furthermore, they often had no wish to re-live the experience. I had a start on writing this book after all the documents my friend Jane had given me. I told Stephen I had a story to tell. So.... the idea for this book was born which became a joint effort and a learning curve for me. I wanted everyone I could reach out to, to learn from Jane's romance scam experience.

We can only thank Jane for sharing her story with us. She was left distraught and broken at the hands of her scammer in a rollercoaster ride of emotion and crippling financial loss that lasted for almost two and a half years.

The hurt lasts considerably longer. Fortunately, Jane had the inner strength to overcome the personal devastation as her wounds started to heal. Today, these events may have started to fade in to the past, but they will never be forgotten. The following story is a true and detailed account of the victim of a romance scam. For those of you who may be unfamiliar with the world of romance scams, Jane hopes that her story will act as a warning to other vulnerable women looking for love online. She told me: "I thought it could never happen to me"

Meet Jane Hollis. This is her story.......

I was born in the San Francisco Bay Area in a time of innocence. You could run around the streets playing until the street lights came on. The only fear we had was being late for dinner.

My early childhood years were happy times, although my parents were divorced when I was a mere two weeks old. In 1955 divorce was not the norm when you wanted out of a bad marriage. You went in different directions, but you stayed together until one or the other died. Attending Catholic School made things a bit difficult due to the teachings about marriage being eternal. I found it easier to say my father was in the military and traveled a lot. It wasn't far from the truth because my parents met in the military service. I never missed out on love of family, at least not in the first twelve years, thanks to my loving grandparents. I have four half sisters and a half brother that I barely know. My father never paid support to my mother and I had no love for him considering he never acknowledged my existence. He took the cowardly way out of responsibility. I often wonder if my insecurities in adult life started at an early age.

I was raised by my devoted Italian grandparents during the first twelve years of my life. We were never rich and if we were poor, I didn't know it. There was always ample food on the table, music and dancing in the house, and a never ending abundance of love. I had six uncles and an aunt, most of which were married. I had several cousins that were like sisters and brothers. In fact, some lived right next door. Before breakfast I was ready to play and would sneak out to their house ready for the day. Most of the time, I would end up having breakfast with my cousins, which was part of the plan anyway. I was an only child, so having them gave me the opportunity to learn the hard way about having to share. All of my uncles and my mom played musical instruments, which gave them the opportunity to have their own band. My uncles were great roll models, as were their wives. I grew up thinking like a man and not like a girl, which is why my best friends are mostly men. I'd rather do things outside than to be stuck in a kitchen, but I was taught to do girlie things too.

There were numerous vacations, sometimes shared with other family members or there were times I had my beloved grandparents to myself. I can remember trips to Atlantic City every summer. My grandma and I really loved the beaches. It's the nature of those born under water signs to crave the atmosphere of sandy beaches and water.

Childhood home in California.

My Childhood Home in California

I remember one particular summer, most of my family spent two weeks in Atlantic City. After dinner each evening we walked the boardwalk and did some shopping. The one evening I can clearly recall was when my aunt (by marriage,) asked me to go look for my uncle. They never had children so they never had it in mind that you don't take your eyes off your children in an over populated area. I ran in to a store to hunt for my uncle, but he was nowhere to be found. I made my exit from the store and there was no sight of my family. I've always been observant to details even at a young age. Here I was, seven years old and my family disappeared. I remembered the name of the hotel was "The Marlboro" which was about four blocks from the boardwalk and I was quite a distance from the city block I needed to walk to. I walked the distance being navigated by memory. The ocean air made me hungry so I stopped to get a sub across from the hotel. I sat and propped my feet up on the banister and proceeded to eat. All of a sudden, three police cars came screaming down the street with sirens blaring in the air. Officers were jumping out everywhere looking worried and hurried. I could see crowds rushing to see what the problem was. I was too hungry to bother, then I looked up and there they were. Both my grandparents crying and carrying on as Italians often do. All I could utter was "uh oh." I stood frozen while I was being interrogated by Atlantic City's finest, with my grandparents using a few expletives in Italian…. words I never understood until I was an adult. Once I regained my composure, I decided to reverse the situation and place the blame on them. "Where the blankety blank have you been?" The shock factor worked well for me. I never swore until that desperate moment.

I sometimes blamed myself for my grandparents dying so soon. I was a holy terror when I was little and there were times I was very headstrong and gave them a run for their money. That is the one thing I wish I could do over. Everything you've ever read about Italian families is so true. We are all passionate with love and just as passionate with arguing. We live life with gusto. Grandma and Grandpa were once thrown out of court for trying to get a divorce on their thirty something anniversary.

Although I loved my grandparents immensely, I always wished I could capture my mother's attention. If I took vacations with my grandparents, I would beg her to come along. She took vacations from work at the same time, but not so she could spend time with me. She dated, went out with friends and cleaned the house. There were many times she would get a day off, but I was lucky to get an hour of her time and often went to bed crying, because it would be another lonely memory.

My grandparents both died within five months of each other and my favourite uncle died six months later, all unexpectedly. Thus began my first experience with heartache. From that year forward, my life changed drastically. I had to grow up and realize the loneliness no child should ever have to experience. I still remained in my grandparents' home, but I was alone all day and sometimes at night. I would go to school without breakfast, occasionally without lunch. At times I could barely wake up in the morning due to getting to bed so late at night. I had homework, laundry and housework to do. My mother would leave notes on how to prepare food and it was my job to carry it through.

After Grandma and Grandpa died, my mother drank heavily. She had mood changes and reminded me daily about how much I looked like my father and if it wasn't for me, she would be driving a Cadillac. The years rolled by rather quickly. There were no more vacations, no more music in the house. But I continued to dance and sing, because it was in my nature to be happy. My grandparents taught me to be happy. My mother used to take me to town and sometimes we'd shop, or sometimes I learned things about her job. I was allowed to talk to customers and conduct business over the phone as though I was an actual employee. I already knew how to type, so I did very well with it.

I first learned about being generous and taking care of our fellow brothers and sisters by watching acts of kindness through my mother and grandmother. I saw this on many occasions and that's when I realized the importance of brotherly love. It trickled down to my children also. We were four generations of giving people just paying it forward.

By the time I was in high school, I banked on the gifts I was given while growing up. I excelled in music, art, sports, gymnastics, dance and most of all, writing and literature. I read all the time, even on vacations. I used my imagination in all directions. I was the neighbourhood drama queen. I got a part in "Oklahoma" and later a part in the "Barber of Seville." I sang, I danced, but I had nobody close in the audience to clap for me, only strangers. Shortly after, I never sang or danced again.

I was 16 years old when I met my first boyfriend. My grandparents had been strict and said I could never date until I was 16. Even though they were no longer here, I still obeyed their wishes. It must have been the strict Catholic School upbringing. By this time I'd spent the past couple years in bars on school nights and weekends. I never drank or smoked and always cared for my health. My mother had a steady boyfriend that had a serious drinking problem. They argued constantly and I felt like the adult. I'd call my mother at work and would ask her to say no when one of my friends would call and ask me to go out with them. Once again, I was an obedient child.

The man I was dating came to my house every night. He also had a drinking problem. By now, this was just a way of life, being surrounded by people who drank to excess. My mother would go to bed and leave us alone. I would give her an evil look when she did that, but I began to think she was hoping I would end up getting pregnant. Then it finally happened. I got raped by this twenty four year old man. Fortunately, it wasn't violent. He didn't know what to do any more than I knew what to do. I'm not sure I wasn't mentally damaged from this experience. I began shutting my mother out of my life. In time I broke away from this rotten man and began making plans to get out of the house and to try to make a new life. Instead of relying on my own resources, I kept depending on a man to get me through the tough spots. So eventually I married a man who I saw as a good long term prospect. I stayed married a very long time because I'm not a quitter. I eventually had children. Life was anything but easy. I went to school, Pepperdine University, and earned more than just one degree. I strived to be the best because I'm a perfectionist. I worked very hard and worked multiple jobs. If I needed something, I earned the money to achieve my goals. My husband knew how to work hard to provide for the family, but he never connected with me or the children. There was no balance. He didn't know how to have fun, and as a parent, he lacked in too many ways. He wasn't a good roll model, nor did he discipline with kindness. He was verbally abusive and was aggressive and demanding. The children were taught to work but he was quite hard on them. On many occasions I should have left him. He cheated with another woman and even though I forgave him, any trust we had between us was gone.

Karma comes in many packages. Sickness came to pay my husband a visit our in the form of Prostate Cancer. I painstakingly researched this slow progressive disease, and learned about the side effects. Its one thing to learn you may never experience making love again, but it's entirely another knowing death can strike at any time when treatment is refused. I wasn't loved enough to fight his corner. It took a while, but eventually this devastating disease took his life. I was alone again, naturally.

Then came the second year of being a widow and I had little experience of living completely alone. I found a career I loved, and signed up for the long haul....literally.

Happier days…. and full of hope and optimism for the future

October 12, 2012

For the first time in my life I was completely alone. Yes, I have a lot of friends, but deep down I was still alone. Changes had to be made. I could not stay in the house indefinitely and I had to begin a new phase in my life. I combined my two loves to make my life perfect. From the first trip taken with my grandparents to my first camera, I fell in love with travel and photography. What better way to spend your life, than with your two loves. The opportunity arose when I was hired to do a six month tour of the mid-west and western states. By early autumn I was on the road and headed west in my camper, with my camera.

The trip went relatively smoothly, apart from nearly getting robbed, and helping a homeless man, and a blowout on the camper. By the time I arrived in Biloxi, Mississippi, in early December, I had received a text message from a stranger on Facebook. He was my age and quite attractive, but I didn't think too much about it. I was preoccupied with looking after another homeless man on the pier that overlooked the Gulf of Mexico.

My new homeless friend, Marvin, played guitar and was serenading me when he broke some guitar strings. He was a bit worried about replacing them. I told him not to worry. I would find some strings. I ran to Wal-mart but had no luck. I finally located a music store, but they had closed just before I arrived. In the meantime, back at Wal-mart, I purchased warm clothing for the coming winter months, a heavy sleeping bag, gloves, and snacks for my friend. When I returned to the pier, I gave him the gifts and reassured him I would get to the music store by morning. I got him two nights at a motel near the pier and told him I would be back by morning for certain. The next day I took him to breakfast, then went about my mission, returning later with a set of new guitar strings. I bid my farewell and hit the road through the states that would eventually lead me to Florida.

December 10, 2012

During the trip to Florida, I re-read the message from the stranger on Facebook. "Hello, sorry to invade your privacy I was searching a friend of mine, I saw your profile and I could not resist, you are beautiful...could you please let me know you?" His name was Dean Simon.

My social media apps were my private world, shared only with close friends and family. I didn't respond to Dean's message straight away due to the caution required regarding strangers online. However, I looked at his picture every day. He had a strong look and a pleasant smile. I've always said, "The eyes are the mirror to the soul," and he was reaching my soul. He had kind eyes. I eventually started writing to him every day, even though I never expected him to respond to my messages. After all, many days went by, without a word, but his message had begun to touch my heart. Part of me wanted to dismiss him, but the lonely part of me begged God to send him to me. Some say, "Be careful what you wish for." We should be happy when God doesn't grant our wishes because he knows each of our hearts.

Every day for several days, I continued to send him messages. I told him a little about myself, and about how I was feeling, my likes and dislikes, and about my decision to let him enter my world on social media, but I also gave him a warning, that if he planned to bother any of my family's children on my Facebook friends list, I would hunt him down, no matter where he is. He assured me that he had no intention of doing so. On December 17th, as I arrived at my destination in Florida, I received a new message from this charming stranger. He had responded to my messages, which now embarrassed me. All he said was "Hi."….as simple as that, but I was shaking inside with excitement. He soon steered me away from Facebook and on to Yahoo messenger. This was a new experience and although I felt uneasy about taking a chance with a stranger online, I was intrigued. I already knew his name was Dean Simon, and I then learned that he had a business called "Simon Ventures", and he claimed to have been an architect for the last twenty years. He was raised by his Grandmother because his parents had died in an auto accident when he was twelve years old and he had lived in Connecticut for the past 2 years. He felt we were soul mates because of so many parallels in our lives. In the days that followed I continued to receive text messages from him. I also found Dean on LinkedIn and eventually he asked me to join it so we could share information about our businesses. He asked me questions about how much money I made on my job, which I felt was a little premature. I figured that some people are just curious, so I tried not to let it bother me. He'd say enough to keep our chats interesting and to keep me wanting to talk to him. I sensed he was a past master in the art of luring women but he said enough of the right things to torture me with a dash of fear of losing him. We were both Roman Catholic, raised by grandparents, both left handed, and he had also attended college. Dean went to Vancouver University, in Nanamo, BC, Canada. He also claimed to have lived in California at some point in his life. We became instant friends, soul mates even, and we really enjoyed our conversations, or at least I did, and I learned that Dean was a current affairs buff and enjoyed stimulating conversation on current affairs, and politics in particular. We often joked about getting jobs with CNN, his favorite news station. He told me all about Michael, his 26 year old son. Michael was his pride and joy, and his best friend.

Dean: The photo that melted Jane's heart

Things were hotting up. Dean declared his love within a week or so. We quickly learned a lot about each other and we asked each other several questions, but he informed me that our texts would have to cease for a while because he was going to Sweden, where he was born. I mentioned my paternal great grandparents were from Sweden and I indicated where, but was surprised at his lack of enthusiasm regarding that bit of coincidental news. We hadn't spoken on the phone yet, but we never pushed anything. We sent texts so infrequently that I soon mentioned to him that in order for this relationship to move forward, we needed communication. Love was like a plant, it needed to be nurtured to survive.

Dean was going to be in Stockholm, Sweden, for the Christmas holidays. He returned the day after New Year. We didn't have contact with each other at all during that week. I felt emptiness while he was gone and I began to wonder if I would ever hear from him again. I felt something was missing. I loved the sweetness in his messages. He made me feel important, which was something I hadn't felt in a very long time. I was hooked.

I walked along the beach and spoke to Dean in my thoughts as though he were walking with me. Everything I did was motivated by him. Everything I put on social media was directed at Dean. I fell asleep lying on the beach as I listened to the waves rolling into the sand. It was a chilly, breezy night in December. Some of my family came searching for me and found me curled into a ball trying to keep warm. I may have had a bug that came out in a vengeance due to the chill that night because I had a fever and was a bit incoherent. They immediately took me to the hospital where I was kept overnight.

Below: Jane's first correspondence exchanged with "Dean"

September 30, 2012
1:25 PM

Dean:
Hello sorry to invade your privacy I was searching a friend of mine, I saw your profile I could not resist you are beautiful...could you please let me know you?

December 14,
11:39 PM

Jane:
I don't usually allow anyone I don't know into my Facebook page because I'm typically a very private person. Thank you for the nice compliment, though. Maybe one day I will learn more about you online. Thank you for contacting me.

December 17,
8:30 PM

Jane:
I noticed your message was dated September 30, 2012. Why am I getting this so late? It was received on December 14th at 10:22 PM.

I've stared at your photos for a few days. You look like a very kind person, and I'm getting a little nutty saying this to a photo that is not going to respond. I'm sorry you are widowed. I know it's difficult at Christmas time. I haven't celebrated Christmas for many years. Someone I loved more than life was killed two weeks before Christmas and I will never celebrate it again. I hope you will be ok. I wonder where you live. Do you have children? I must be losing my mind. I'm talking to a photo as though it is my best friend.

December 18,
6:27 PM

Jane:
I doubt you will ever be back to Facebook again, so I may talk a while tonight. This way you will remain in the inbox. Otherwise, you will be tossed to the bottom of the page and will no longer be visible to me.

It would have been nice to have you here when I began my tour. I met so many nice people, took thousands of photos and had a few scares. For instance, getting stranded in the mountains in California, lost in Death Valley and nearly robbed in New Mexico by three characters. You missed all that, all because of late email service.

Jane:
I'm back again. You will think twice before asking to know someone ever again. You never dreamed it would be so entertaining, did you? Where should we get started, you're the one that wanted to know. You already read that I can speak and understand Italian. The truth is I understand it better then I speak it. I can get by if I go to Italy. I still have some family that lives there that I keep in touch with. It's my plan after I finish my tour of America. I still have to visit New England for the second time.

My best friends are men because we always talked about every day things like sports and cars, other than shopping, hair styles and which guy has the cutest butt. I don't enjoy shopping that much. I make a list and go for my target, then head home as quickly as possible. I don't spend a lot of time primping and being a fluff chick unless I'm forced into it, like to go to a wedding or a funeral to attend. I was blessed or cursed with thick, curly hair, so I don't linger in a salon for days. I'm happy with what my creator gave me to work with.

My first love is my camera and I want the world to see what I see. My other loves are family, but I don't place them first because I don't think that's healthy. We all have our own life to live. I don't really get too attached to anyone because in the end you wind up getting hurt. As I mentioned, my best friends are men, but it is only a friendship. I don't have to have a man in my life to be happy. I just want the friendships. They mean a lot to me.

December 20,
8:34 PM

I'm doing it again. I'm staring at a photo that belongs to an imaginary, non existent person. You really do smile with your eyes. I like that. This is starting to hurt a little because now I want to meet you. It wasn't supposed to go this way.

December 21,
11:52 AM

Dean: Hi

Jane: Now I'm really embarrassed.

Dean Simon. Jane began to feel closer to him with every passing day.

Inside Jane's camper.
Home from home for six months on the road

Photos and memories from Jane's road trip.... as her involvement with Dean started to overshadow everything else in her life

(Above) Mt Rushmore

(Below) Montana

The San Antonio Riverwalk

The Riverwalk is lined with shops and eateries on walkways beneath the city streets of San Antonio. The walk has gradually expanded to 5 miles of winding walking areas and is open 365 days of the year.

The Battle of the Alamo (February 23-March 6, 1836)

....are dates that are synonymous with the 13 day siege. Mexican troops led by Santa Anna, launched an assault on the Alamo Mission, near San Antonio Bexar, which is now the modern day San Antonio. Texas volunteers came to the Alamo to protect the mission, but were soon outnumbered. While some Texans surrendered, they were immediately executed. The Alamo is one of the most visited tourist attractions in the U.S.

Mount Saint Helens

The last eruption for this stratovolcano, named after a British diplomat, Lord St. Helens, was on July 10th, 2008. This mountain, with the elevation of 8,366 feet, erupted in 1980. On May 18, 1980, the deadliest and most economically destructive volcanic event in United States history took place. Fifty seven people were killed; 250 homes were destroyed, 475 miles of railways, and 185 miles of highway were destroyed.

Jane recalls: In October of 2012, I had the privilege of meeting a gentleman that participated in the rebirth of Mount St. Helens. He and several volunteers planted new trees to replace those destroyed in the lava fire. I gained first hand knowledge of the events that transpired that day.

Murrah Bomb Blast memorial Oklahoma City, Oklahoma

Reflecting Pool:

A thin layer of water flows over polished black granite to form the pool, which runs east to west down the centre of the Memorial on what was once Fifth Street. Although the pool is flowing, visitors are able to see a mirror image of themselves in the water. Visitors seeing their reflections are said to be seeing "someone changed forever by what happened here." Jane remembers: This was very true for me. This was the start of a very depressing period in my life.

Field of Empty Chairs:

168 empty chairs hand-crafted from glass, bronze, and stone represent those who lost their lives, with a name etched in the glass base of each chair. They sit on the site where the Murrah Building once stood. The chairs represent the empty chairs at the dinner tables of the victims' families. The chairs are arranged in nine rows to symbolize the nine floors of the building; each person's chair is on the row (or the floor) on which the person worked or was located when the bomb went off. The chairs are also grouped according to the blast pattern, with the most chairs nearest the most heavily damaged portion of the building. The westernmost column of five chairs represents the five people who died but were not in the Murrah Building (two in the Water Resources Board building, one in the Athenian Building, one outside near the building, and one rescuer). The 19 smaller chairs represent the children killed in the bombing. Three unborn children died along with their mothers, and they are listed on their mother's chairs beneath their mother's names.

OFF TO SWEDEN

I really like Dean a lot. He's rapidly becoming my best friend. He seems to know me so well. If I don't feel well, he texts me as though he has a sense something isn't right. It's all happening so fast. Dean said he is tired of being alone and wants me to be in his life forever. He has been a widower for many years, since his son Michael was two years old. He asked me to go to Sweden with him. As much as I want to go, I can't be irresponsible with my job or my family. I reluctantly declined.

It was on December 20th 2012 before I heard his voice for the first time. We text all the time, but today I had to hear his voice. I found that I could barely understand him due to his deep accent, but I listened intently. We can work it out. Tomorrow he leaves for Sweden, his homeland. I wish he would change his mind. Without his family, why would he feel the need to go there? Michael is working in England, so why not go there instead? I felt so empty without my Dean. It's now 10:00am, and time now for him to board his plane. I don't want to be selfish so I told him to have a good time. Part of me wonders if he has a lover in Sweden. He's an only child and I'm certain there has to be someone he wants to visit there.

It seems like weeks have gone by without a word, yet it's only been days. I hope Dean hasn't forgotten me. I can't eat and I can't sleep. I miss him so much and I feel so alone again. I'm so used to his being there when I want to talk to him.

Its Christmas morning and I wake up to a silly Christmas Carol written to me by Dean. I almost feel angry that he is so cheerful when I feel so miserable without him. I feel as though he doesn't miss me as much as I miss him. I stare at his photo all the time. He's consuming my every thought. I've never experienced real love. Is this normal to feel this attached to another human being? Dean has stirred so many emotions I've never felt before. He says all the right things when I need to hear them most. How can I ever be angry at him with his cheerful sweetness? I forgive you Dean. I will always forgive you.

January, 2013
It's January 3rd and my Dean is home at last. Things will be normal once again. I'm thankful he's safely back in America. I'm not eating much. Months passed. I never worried so much over one person.

I felt the same feelings of elation every time Dean contacted me, and one day he told me he had a job offer and is working on a proposal which will be presented in New York City. I suppose I have to get used to this way of life. Dean was an architect, after all. There is so much growth and construction here in the U.S. Of course, he was hired to do the job.

Dean asked me to marry him by the end of 2013 and without a second thought I said yes. When he returns from this job he is going to be able to fulfil his dream to open his own Art Gallery. The coming New Year will be my happiest year ever. He fills my heart with joy and we have so much living to do. We are a family.

My sweet love is gone again. I feel resentful when he leaves. It's his job and I have to stop acting like a spoiled child. I have to accept his life as he has to accept mine. Dean left for New York on the 5th of January and now it's the 10th. I haven't heard from him and I'm very concerned about his well-being. I have a strong feeling something is very wrong. He is at a hotel in the city, but the question is where? I've called him, sent E-mails, yet no answer. It makes me feel as though Dean is playing a very cruel joke. How does a man in love behave this way? He has asked me to inform him when I go places, yet he disappears for days without a word. I've been crying and I go to sleep with his picture next to me. Rain or shine I walk endlessly. I want to call the police about my missing man, but I'm afraid I'll come across as some kind of lunatic. Who really falls in love online anyway? I'll try to forget him …but he is in my blood. He's become a habit and he's a part of me now. I can no longer look back. I can't keep food down. I feel sick. I am always waiting. I feel the walls closing in on me. Why does loving someone have to hurt so much? I have to get back on the road again. I can't avoid working. I'll lose myself in my work. It's all I have for now.

Dean's been in New York for 8 days and once again….he's gone quiet. No calls, no contact. I decided to try and call him one last time. He finally answered his phone and all I could do was cry uncontrollably. I could barely speak. I've been driven to become so needy, the very type of woman I loathed. Then again, why shouldn't I be needy? I'm investing my life in this relationship. I was so angry because he never seemed to notice the emotional turmoil I was suffering. I'm beginning to believe he enjoys creating all this uncertainty that is festering inside of me. He's simply playing hard to get. Dean claims to have been sick and said I need to be patient. Yet I always feel as though I'm not enough for him. A simple phone call…is that too much to ask? He could have called somewhere along the line. Anything is better than nothing.

Dean got the job he was after and is now going to South Africa, to Cape Town. This will be his last job. When the job is complete he will come home to begin our new life together. He wants to leave a legacy and will be able to give us a wonderful life. I never cared about money, just the life I wanted with Dean. Despite trying to convince him he could do his work here, there is never a clear answer from this complex man. I just have to hope that everything comes together as planned.

Dean left for South Africa the following day and I was not surprised. He had no sooner unpacked… then was off again. This time I made him promise he would let me know he arrived safely in South Africa. He complied and I was relieved. He arrived on the 22nd of January and sent me a quick text. After 9/11, I worried about flights to foreign countries. I have never been lucky with love and planning a future wedding seemed more like a fantasy than a reality.

Dean promised me he would be home in a couple months and not to feel sad because the time would go quickly. He encouraged me to take an interest in his work and he sent me a copy of the blueprints showing his beautiful design for a shopping mall the size of a city block. He would be renovating a disused structure. I never believed he would be home in a couple of months because this was going to be a major job and this type of project is not an overnight one. Construction of this type was no mystery to me because I was married to a construction engineer. I start to feel like a part of Dean's life. Once again, I'm feeling comfortable. I know the relationship is complicated due to the miles between us, but we are meant to be and no one will destroy that. I want to trust him, yet part of me doubts his feelings and intentions. Again, every time I call him, there is no answer. I text him and he says wait ten minutes and I'll call you. He's always at a meeting or there is someone in his office. If I don't answer my phone, he gets angry. He complains when I go on the internet and accuses me of looking for other men.

We text or talk every day and I seem to have a clearer understanding of his personality. I sometimes feel that he isn't the same person as the one I first met, but can't be sure. I have mixed emotions. Sometimes I find myself sleeping more than I should. I know it's an escape from reality.

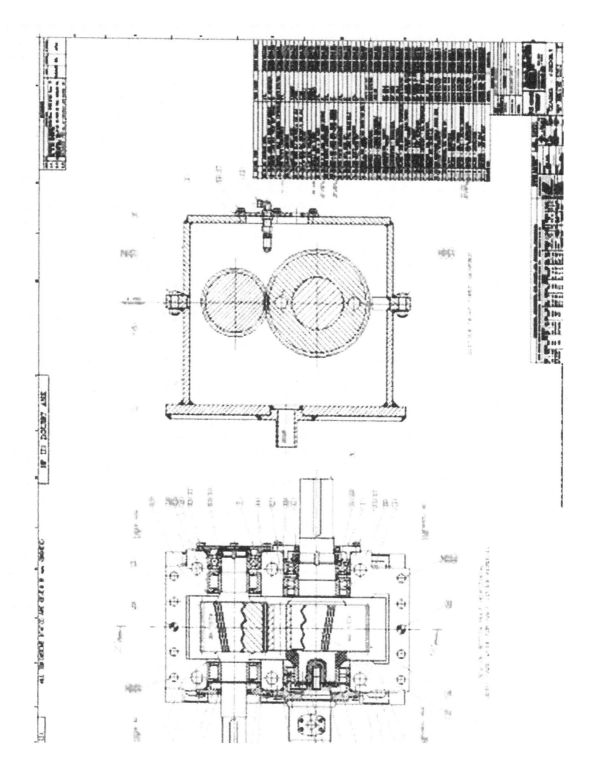

Dean's blueprints for his new "building project." Impressive to those who know little about architectural design. Dean's ambitions and his knowledge on the subject seemed to have the desired affect when it came to making a lasting impression on someone. Here is a man who is not only charming and good looking….he also has a" lucrative career".

Simon Ventures

Geographic Presence

Preferred Situations

Preferred Transactions

Investment Philosophy

Portfolio Companies

Biographies

Our Commitment

Contact Information

Simon Ventures, LP is a private equity investment firm, established in 1996, for the purpose of creating a diversified portfolio of growth opportunities. While unconstrained as to the type of business, it typically pursues companies having enterprise values from $5 million to $50 million with growth potential that may be unlocked through greater access to capital. Simon Ventures relies on management to execute the day-to-day operating plan, but makes its experience, relationships and capital available to enhance the portfolio company's performance. The firm emphasizes entrepreneurial spirit and therefore a substantial portion of management compensation relates to the ultimate success of the company.

Simon Ventures' investment professionals have a unique combination of financial and operational expertise. Leveraging both sets of skills, the firm has made successful investments in a variety of businesses, including: manufacturing, service and distribution.

Geographic Presence | Preferred Situations | Preferred Transactions
Investment Philosophy | Portfolio Companies | Biographies
Our Commitment | Contact Information | Home

Simon Ventures, LP

Various ads, details, and e-mails regarding "Dean's business" were sent to Jane to "prove" that Simon Ventures was a legitimate company. Although this company is registered and appears to exist....it has nothing whatsoever to do with "Dean Simon."

Academyrox Two Limited 100% owned by SWWI. (f/k/a Cyrk/Tonkin Europe Limited)	United Kingdom
Super Premium Limited Islands 100% owned by SWWI	British Virgin
Global Sourcing, Inc. Islands 100% owned by SWWI (f/k/a Cyrk Far East, Inc.)	British Virgin
Global Sourcing (HK) Limited 100% owned by Global Sourcing, Inc. (f/k/a Cyrk (H.K.) Limited)	Hong Kong
Simon Worldwide (Canada), Inc. 100% owned by SWWI (f/k/a Cyrk Marketing Services, Inc.)	Canada
Simonww.com, Inc. 100% owned by SWWI (f/k/a Cyrk.com, Inc.)	Delaware
Simon Marketing, Inc. 100% owned by SWWI	Delaware
Simon Marketing (Hong Kong) Limited 100% owned by Simon Marketing, Inc.	Hong Kong
Simon Ventures, Inc. 100% owned by Simon Marketing, Inc.	California
Simon Marketing Consulting (Canada) Limited 100% owned by Simon Ventures, Inc.	Canada
. Simon Ventures International	United Kingdom

February, 2013

I am anxiously awaiting a phone call from Dean. I know he's very busy and we've only been able to text occasionally these days because he complains his internet is so bad. I've driven all day and headed north, but stopping to do photo shoots along the way.

By midnight, I had given up on him calling me. At 3am. I was awakened by a man crying and I could hear trembling in his voice. My heart was in my throat. I repeatedly said hello and never got an answer, at least not until I got very angry. All I had in my mind was the thought something happened to Dean and how would I get him home for me to take care of him? "God, please don't let anything happen to him."

Michael

I've seen so many photos of Michael that I would know him anywhere. He has his fathers smile and that mischievous gleam in his eyes. He is strong, muscular, and healthy in appearance. Michael, very much like his father, loves motorcycles and boating. Dean and Michael are best friends, which is obvious in the photos.

Michael lives in England where he had studied at university and is currently employed with an investment firm…. a company whose name was never mentioned. I'm pleased that Dean has told Michael about us and that he is happy about the entire situation. He has told his dad in no uncertain terms, that he had better be good to me and not to do anything to "screw this up."

Now I have Dean sobbing on the other end of this phone because his best friend, his son, his only child, has been seriously injured in a motorcycle accident. He is upset because he can't be in two places at once. He can't leave this project so he is maintaining an open line of communication with Michael's doctor. He said Michael has a habit of riding at high speeds and tends to be too reckless. He slid on a slick oily patch on the road. The doctors told Dean that Michael's legs are crushed and he will likely never walk again, if he lives through the night. Dean said he can't leave Cape Town to go to England, especially at this crucial point in this project he has started and he's now getting frustrated with being there. He asked me to research doctors specializing in this kind of medical issue and to let him know what I come across. I could feel Dean's pain. I was to find a plastic surgeon and an orthopaedic surgeon to fix Michael. We would have to find them here, or in Connecticut where I would eventually be moving to.

After ending the call with Dean, I broke down and cried. I had to be strong for him. I could only weep for the pain Dean was going through. I prayed like I have never prayed before. Michael has referred to me as "Mom" more than once, while talking to his dad about me. I begged God to take my life instead. Dean lived for Michael. It would destroy him to lose his son. I felt he was my son too.

The next few days I could hear the frustration mounting in Dean's voice, and I fully understood. Michael was coherent and appeared to be doing a bit better. I felt it was a miracle. Dean was concerned because Michael was becoming depressed, which is quite understandable. For many months after the night of the accident, Michael kept sinking deeper into depression. As he had been so athletic and active in the past, I know he will have difficulty accepting the fact he may spend the rest of his life in a wheel chair. I researched endlessly and found a doctor, then read about devices to help a person walk again through computers. I also learned he would have to have extensive surgeries to repair some of the damage. I asked Dean if Michael had a wheelchair. He said the hospital has one for him while there in the hospital, however he will need to get him one to use at home. He said he didn't have the money with him while he is in Cape Town. I told him I couldn't help him because I was on this tour. At that moment I got a return text from what seemed to be from the devil himself. He said he didn't need my help. I knew he was too proud to ask. Michael was supposedly put on suicide watch at the hospital. Although, I admit I'm a bit perplexed by that happening. How is a person at risk of suicide when he has no mobility?

I gave some careful thought for a special birthday gift for Michael. His birthday was on February 24th and Dean's birthday was on February 14th. I'll be late getting these gifts to them, because I have to wait until I arrive home. I know what Michael will truly enjoy and I will be able to communicate with him. His phone was destroyed in the accident and I've decided to purchase an iPad for him. I want to spoil him because he has lost so much at such a young age. I'm going to become the mother he never had.

Michael's birth mother chose her lover and left her son behind for Dean to raise. She never saw her son again, that is until she discovered she was dying of cancer and had only a short time left to live. She came back home to die, with Dean summoned to take care of her until she passed away. She died in his arms. He has had to endure so much sadness in his life. I'm more determined than ever, to change his life for the better. I love him more each day, even more so for his kindness toward the woman that broke his heart so long ago.

I have now arrived home a little earlier than expected. My goals were completed on this tour and I was emotionally drained due to all that had transpired within these past months. I'm battling with my own demons right now. I'm beginning to feel depressed. I constantly worry about Dean and Michael. I am thinking of the unfairness in life.

Below: Two of the messages exchanged between Dean and Jane regarding "Michael's motorcycle accident"

I am looking down at you as you are sleeping, thanking God for putting us together and praying to he will always have his angels watch over you. Sleep well my husband. My heart remains with you now and always. I love you more today than yesterday.

Jan 25, 6:00 PM

My wife I can't sleep

I'm here with you sweetheart. Tell me what's troubling you?

They call me from England my son had a terrible accident..

Lol

 What happen to your glasses ?

> I fell asleep wearing them and
> they are in this
> bed....somewhere

 Michael will never be able to
walk again

Jan 26, 5:47 AM

> Oh dean I'm so sorry.

 I've to go there because doctor
said he need surgery

> At least he is alive yes my
> darling you must go there

Dean.... And "son" Michael

Michael and I have written numerous E-Mails and sent photos to one another for several days now. I try to keep things light and cheerful. I look forward to all the letters and he sounds quite cheerful as we write. He continuously tells me his dad is so happy about having a woman in his life that is willing to stand by him through all things good and bad. I feel as though my family is adjusting to the circumstances. These two are so close they even talk alike. My thoughts are to bring Michael here to live, so we can give him the care he needs and we can be close to him.

After I'm settled at home, I have to get the birthday gifts sent. I'm happy to be able to cheer up Michael in some way. Dean wants me to look for a large ranch style home for us to live. He plans to come "home" soon. I can't stop smiling at the thought that my dream of happiness with Dean and our son Michael will soon become a reality

I'm so happy my deposits came in for the work I've completed this past 6 months, because my two loves will have beautiful gifts from me. I've selected a gold chain and pendant and I've had it engraved, "To my man in the photo." I sent miscellaneous things he needed. Dean said he needed vitamins because he was feeling very tired all the time and these I sent together with music that I put together that I thought he would like. I took a two hour trip to the Apple store to get the iPad and a cell phone I had promised Michael. It took Dean a couple weeks before he came up with an address to send these things. Just in shipping, taxes and duties, my fee was more than $600.00. The gold chain and pendant, plus engraving cost about the same. Let's not even discuss the cost of the iPad. I finally got an address for Dean's translator's home in Johannesburg, South Africa. That was an interesting coincidence, because I had a new friend from Johannesburg.

I had unexpectedly made an acquaintance with a charming lady called Ajay while on my camper tour, before my association with Dean started. She and I decided to keep in touch throughout the remainder of my trip. She was pleasant, chatty, and we became close, and we found that we had much in common. She had a friend in her group of friends on Facebook who made contact with me via Ajay's friends list. I accepted his friend request and thought little of it, and we poked each other through Facebook on several occasions (as you do for fun). He claimed to be a minister with an Apostolic Church, but unbeknown to me at the time, this was probably my first encounter with Dean, before Dean officially came on the scene. For all intents and purposes, I was simply exchanging pokes with a faceless stranger. All of a sudden the pokes ceased and he was gone from Ajay's, and also my own friends list. Out of the blue came the friend request from Dean Simon. Once again, I thought little of it. I'm sure that most Facebook users accept friend requests because the person behind the request comes across as honest, and possibly interesting, or they simply like the profile photo. A short time later, after we had acquainted ourselves with each other and started to exchange messages I told Ajay about this wonderful man I'd started chatting with… even though Dean wanted me to keep him a secret for now. Ajay was happy for me but she thought Dean was a little suspect.

Jane went on to explain: "I feel that the Church Minister was actually Dean because he took himself off Ajay's friend list and he stopped poking me. He did it frequently then stopped. Then suddenly Dean Simon came along. He had obviously singled me out and maybe saw me as someone who could be easily manipulated. I think Ajay may know something because I showed her Dean's photo and she said he was a player. I asked her if she knew him and she said no. I think that may have been a lie because Dean got angry at me for confiding in someone about him. How would he have known that unless Ajay had told him?"

The E-mails are now few and far between, which concerned me. Dean said he never forwarded Michael's gifts to him because he is in the mental health unit due to his acting out and his constant depression. Dean isn't exactly tolerant of another person's weaknesses but I'm impatient to see that Michael gets his gifts. One afternoon, I asked Dean to talk to me about Michael. I needed to know if his health was improving and if I could call him. Dean gave me a phone number to call and speak to Michael's doctor, which I thought was a little odd, especially since I wasn't a blood relative. Dean said if I want to know, I had to call. I decided to let it go. I am not going to push this since Dean was obviously very upset about my asking questions. Our conversations frequently turn into arguments. He works until the early hours of the morning and still tries to keep up with the time changes in my part of the world. He works late due to the safety issues with traffic. After his anger subsides, he tells me his is so tired and wants to come home. I know his son means everything to him, so I always forgive him.

Dean and Michael. "The perfect father and son"

Good morning mom how was your night? Thank you for all the support you've been giving my dad God almighty will continue to bless you. I hope he forgive me for everything he's going through now just because of me is a good father he always give me anything ask for I'm proud of him very hard working father he always want the best for me.

Dad love you so much he told me one day he will never his life again without you, I hope you take me as your son is a pity I never had a mother to take care of me he's the only one doing everything for me I will be very happy if you can accept me as your son and I promise to be a good son.

Your Son,

Michael.

To Michael Simon
Feb. 18, 2013

Dear Michael,

Today the sun is finally shining and that may be because I am seeing the light at the end of the tunnel. Your father is getting closer to coming to you Michael. He has worked so hard to get this job finished so he can be with you.

Michael, I had a dream of the moment I finally meet you. It is as though I'm awaiting the birth of my child. It brings tears to my eyes thinking about it. I will be a loving mother to you. I'll make you laugh and will keep you busy. I may even make you angry at times. Parents are good about making their children angry once in a while. It will be good for us to be together.

One day you'll meet the rest of your new family, which may be a little overwhelming at first. I know they overwhelm me sometimes. They've always outnumbered me Michael. Some day I'll tell you about some of the tricks they've played on me throughout they're lives. I hope each day makes you stronger than the last.

I bought your iPad and as soon as your dad sends me an address, I'll send it along. I would be far more comfortable sending it to you, but your dad said he would not want to gamble on it falling into the wrong hands. He wants to bring it with him when he comes to England. Just be patient honey and it will get to you soon. Your father's birthday gift will be enclosed in the package.

I look at your photo your father sent me of the two of you. You look so much like him. I am blessed with two angels, not just one. Be strong Michael. You are much loved by your father and your mother. We will be together one day, as a beautiful family.

From your loving mother.

Feb 19, 2013

Dear Michael,

I spoke to your father last night and I had the need to write to you this morning. I don't know if you are reading my letters, but I will still send them in hopes you are getting them. I just want you to know my son, that I am very worried about you and that you are not alone. It wasn't all that long ago I felt as though my own life wasn't worth living. Then I met your wonderful father. When A door is closed, God opens a window. There will be a purpose for you Michael, you have to find what it is. In the meantime, I'm here for you and I don't want to lose you, when I just found you. No one's life is perfect, but we have to make it the best we can. My joy has always come from photography that I enjoy sharing with others. It is the one thing that has kept me going for a long time. I have hopes that one day, you and I can take pictures together and maybe travel to different places to get them. Once you see the beauty you can put on paper, you may enjoy it as a hobby.

Just remember Michael, I am here for you if you want to write to me. I don't have all the answers, just experience in life. Sometimes talking things through can help us see where we want to be.

I love you.
Mom

me
To
Michael Simon

Feb 20, 2013

Dear Michael,

On Saturday, February 23, I will drive to Pittsburgh to pick up your iPhone, there again, depending on the weather. Tonight I am going to get your iPad wrapped and ready for shipping FedEx. I can't wait until you receive it. You will love it. It's easy to use but a lot to learn about it. I'm sure you probably know more about them than I do. I'll let you know the day it gets shipped and a tracking number so you will know where it is. Of course, I'm still waiting for your Dad to get me a shipping address. Between the two of us, we should nag him to death until he decides where I should send this. Lol.

I love you and I'm so excited to get this to you.

me
To
Michael Simon

Feb 22, 2013

Dear Michael,

I'm not sure I know what is going on between you and your Dad, but I hope it has been resolved by now. I never got to talk to him last night and I think it's because he was so tired. He was a little upset. Michael, you and I must work together at trying to be patient with your Dad because he is getting exhausted. He works so many hours and still tries to keep up with the two of us. I wish he wouldn't work that way because if he ever got sick or hurt I would surely die without him.

I'm going in the morning to get the phone and on Monday I hope to send everything to your Dad. I'm hoping before long you will have your gifts at last. I know you are eager to get these things, and rightfully so. As they say, all good things are worth waiting for. You will have many hours of joy coming to you soon.

Michael, you are truly loved by your father. He always worries about you and so do I. I feel as though I have known you all my life. I could not love you more if I gave birth to you. You are a part of your father and I love him more than my own life. Therefore I love you the same way.

Be patient my sweet son. Good things will come soon.
Love,
Mom

me

Feb 24, 2013
Dear Michael,

Once again, your Mom is chatty. I can't help it because I love having my son to write to.

I have had a busy day today taking care of a few things in another town. It took several hours, but now I'm home. I wanted to write before a new day began. I want to write to you everyday.

Michael, why did we all come together to be a family? What was God's plan for us? In my wildest dreams, I never looked for any of this to happen. For a very long time, I would dream of a man that would come to me in my dreams many nights. I did not know him, but he said he loved me. When I woke up in the morning I would cry because he was gone. Maybe weeks later, he would come to me again. Then one night I got on Facebook, (my Facebook was closed to the outside world.) there he was, the man in my dreams. He wanted to know me. At first I said no. The longer I stared at his picture, the more I felt he was very familiar. I saw the gentleness in his eyes and his smile. I started to write things to the man in the photo. Soon, it was getting uncontrollable. Michael. I was begging God bring him to me. I never got an answer from the man in the photo until 2 weeks went by that I had been writing. I felt embarrassed because I wrote so many things I never thought he would see regarding my feelings. I know children don't want to hear this love stuff about their parents, but I have no one else to talk to about this. Michael, I kneel at my bed every night and I thank God for this man. The tears are running down my cheek, even as I write this. I will never hurt this beautiful man that has stolen my heart. I would give up my own life to save his. I have never loved another man like this. Then one day he told me he had you and I felt my heart would explode. It was more love pouring into my heart. How could I have so much given to me all at once? When your Dad told me about your accident, I wanted to scream. I was helpless because you were in England and I was stuck here on a photo assignment. I wanted to comfort my 2 men, and couldn't be with either of you. I was angry at God because I couldn't stand the thoughts of him taking you from me before I had the chance to meet you. Now I am able to have my son. I need you in my life Michael. You and my Dean are an answer to my prayer. I have a wonderful son and a husband all at once. I'm truly blessed.

With all my love,

Mom

me
To
deansimon55@aol.com

Mar 5, 2013
Dear Dean,
Before I write to Michael, I wanted to write to you. These past months In our relationship has been bittersweet. I fell in love with you and nothing will ever change that.

While I was traveling all those miles, I fought being in a deep depression, which is something not uncommon when traveling that many miles and for so long a time. Many people that I know that are also "Road Warriors", have gone through the same kind of depression. It is a feeling of isolation that is overwhelming. I loved what I did and I loved being home. These two things battled each other. When I met you, the depression escalated even more because we connected immediately, but I felt it was hurting me more than you because you at least had other things in your life and I was still isolated from the world. I cried more than I ever did in my entire life. All I knew was that I loved you, could not explain it and I was living in my own hell because I wasn't really sure how i should handle this relationship. The music I listened to was pure torture. I kept this all secret and had no one to talk to of this feeling I had. When you were sick with the flu in New York, with no one to take care of you, and not knowing where you were, I was afraid I would never hear your voice again. My heart was breaking. I even thought I might commit suicide, that is how depressed and fragile I became. I never wanted you to know it had gotten that bad. I knew I had to end this trip and very soon. I used my friend's accident to get home early. Yes I was concerned for her, but more for me. I was very close, so much that I called my priest to talk to him about how I was feeling. He never knew I was feeling this way because I loved you.

Since then, our love has grown deeper and we are closer than ever. I have never tried to be someone that I am not. This is the person I am Dean. I love deeply and passionately, my pain is real when I am sad. I have always dreamed one day my love would come to me, and he has. I'm have never lived a sophisticated life so I have to say, I'm old fashioned to a point, I'm not afraid to express my feelings for those I care about. I hug my friends, my children kiss me hello and good bye, I will always tell you what I feel and what I do. I hide nothing. Although I have many people that I am friends with, my husband is my best friend and the only person I ever confide in. I have always been the kind of person that would center my life around my husband, my children and my home, in that order.

I wanted you to know all of this because if you want anyone different, then we need to work this out now. Just know, you will be the one I take care of first. I want to always be able to take care of you when you are sick and laugh and love with you when you are well. You will never be alone again.

The next few months are going to be difficult for us. This time I will be the one committed to finish a job. I will enjoy this job and I will be available as much as I possibly can. On October 1st, I go on the road again and truthfully, I don't want to do it and I'm considering settling the issue and getting out of going. We can talk about that later. There are many things we need to plan and talk about, but it should be done when we can be together or when we can talk in the states. These phone calls are outrageous.

We must consider Michael when we plan our lives. He will be very important In all our decisions. I never want his feelings ignored. We also have to take careful thought in how we handle these plans we make. I also have to consider the feelings of our grandchildren and how this will effect them. I have no doubt they will all love you when they know you. Family is important to me and I don't want to do something to change how they feel about me. Our love comes first, but we have to act wisely.

Mar 10, 2013
Dear Michael,

I hope you are doing well. Michael, I just wish you were at a place that I could come and spend time with you and we could talk and laugh and get to know each other better.

I miss your Dad so much. I don't know what to do anymore. I can't go to him until I can get my passport. I can't go to you either, for the same reason. It's difficult for both of us Michael. I wish he could look inside my head and my heart so he could understand my needs. Sometimes he gets so quiet and fails to respond to my mail. What he doesn't understand is, by doing this, it hurts me so much, because I need his words of love and encouragement every day. I shouldn't be telling you these things because you have your own concerns. You know your father better than I do, but I also love him as much as you do. I'm sorry Michael, I'm supposed to be consoling you, and here I am crying on your shoulder. I have no one that I can go to with these things. You are the only person that I have. I tell your Dad also, but it seems at times he gets so worried, he grows silent. I want be strong for him because I am so proud of him and what he is doing. I want him to finish his work and then we can spend the rest of our lives living our dream. I will wait for an eternity if necessary, but I have to have his words of love to keep me steadfast.

I just sent two other letters that I wrote two or three days ago. Both times I fell asleep before I could finish them.

I have tracked the FedEx package and it appears it is in customs already. This was fast. It's supposed to be delivered by Tuesday afternoon. I hope your father can arrange to get it without a problem.

Michael, I'm so happy you are in my life.
I love both my men.
Always,
Mom.

Mar 21, 2013

My Husband, my Love,

There are no words I can give you that can explain what I feel. Time moves so slowly and is so unkind and unmerciful. It takes no pity on us and is uncaring. The only way I can manage these days is to sleep, because sleep takes me to you. Tears are my constant companion. I know for everything in life there is a reason. I know I have to wait for God's time for us to be together. So I will remain patient.

I want you to know that I live for the minutes we share writing to each other. It eases the pain of separation. It continues to give me hope. None of this is easy because the heart wants what the heart wants, and my heart wants you. I sometimes ask myself, if I would have known how long I would have to wait or how much heartache this would be, would I have asked God to give you to me? Yes, I would do it again, because I know one day, we will have all our heart desires. I'm not speaking of material things. I'm speaking of something more valuable. We will be side by side taking care of each other and living a life full of love, devotion and care for each other. We will take care of Michael, Dean.

Once this long wait is over, you will understand one thing certain. You will know that I stayed with you through this. I waited for you no matter the time it took. By doing so, you will know I would never leave you after all this. I stayed through the bad times. I'll be there in the good times. You have to know, I never ran away when you told me about Michael, I will never run later. You are the man I want to love and honor all of my life. You are the only man I was created for. God is grooming me for a life suited to my needs. I need to care for someone. This is who I am. You are the someone. Michael is the someone. God knew what you needed. You needed to be loved and cared for. You were broken and now I want to mend your heart. Michael needs a mother. I want to be his mother. I will love him with all I have to give. I want you to believe and understand that. I told you once, love trickles down. Because I love you, I naturally love Michael.

Good things come to those that wait. It's all in God's good time.

I love you.

St. Christopher was the "patron saint of travelers". Jane quotes: " Dean and I both had Catholic backgrounds and I felt it appropriate to buy him this medal and chain for his birthday. The back of the medal reads, "To man in photo. Love, Jane"

Dean's phone: One of many gifts sent over a period of several months.
Michael was also sent a phone, and an ipad, thus enabling Dean, Michael,
and Jane to keep in constant touch with each other.

TEMPER TEMPER

April, 2013

Tonight when I spoke to Dean, he seemed distracted and I can hear loud noises in the background, with yelling and shouting. It wasn't long before Dean was shouting and yelling loudly in return. By now he was speaking fluent Swahili. He muffled the phone and I couldn't understand what was happening. He said he'd call me back as quickly as he could. I remember him saying one of his employees was throwing a tantrum. Of course it worried me. I begged him to be very careful. I told him I wanted him out of that God forsaken place.

The following day, Dean explained the incident that took place at the project the night before. It seems there was a worker that decided to take his frustration out on the machinery he was working with. It was rented for ditch digging at the site. Dean repaired the machinery as well as could be expected and continued to work with it after telling his employee to go home. Dean then fired him and told him not to return. I feared the angry worker might return. I thought he'd come back with a vengeance. Dean acknowledged I might be right but made no further comment.

For the next couple of weeks Dean and I seemed close again. He was more cheerful, which made me more cheerful. We made plans for our future together, although I had given up looking for a house and virtually gave up on the possibility that his son Michael would ever be a part of our family. I really didn't know in which direction this was all heading, but I also hung on to the hope that everything would work out just fine. Dean's project was going well and progressing better than he ever expected. I would still prepare the house for Michael, but I knew better than to expect too much. He will be a handful if he does get home, but together we can do anything within reason.

I got a call from Dean. He has had a lot of pain in his shoulder, arm and wrist. The pain isn't going away and he is starting to feel sick. I told him to try to sleep and maybe in a few hours he will begin to feel better.

On the following day, at 5 a.m., my phone rang and the stranger on the phone informed me with the news Dean was taken to the hospital, which would be afternoon in that part of the world. He identified himself as Dean's translator, Ajeniya Afolabi. He told me that I was to call Dean's doctor for information about Dean's health. The translator and the doctor both informed me of the seriousness of what had happened to Dean. My heart felt like it was about to break in a million pieces.

It seems that two very big men broke into Dean's apartment and tore the place apart, destroying everything in sight. As Dean approached the men when he ascended the stairs, they grabbed him and pushed him down the steps, causing severe injuries. They also threw his computer down the stairs. Both the translator and the doctor (Dr Stephen Muller) told me that he would need surgery immediately, which would cost $900.00. That didn't seem like an awful lot of money for surgery, but I read somewhere that hospitals are quite good in South Africa. Dean offered up his passport as security in exchange for the money that he soon hoped to obtain. He assured them that he would not leave the country until the bill for his treatment was paid in full. I looked up the doctor and the hospital online, but there was no record of them. I did however phone the number I was given for the doctor and found him to be quite rude. I asked for his medical qualifications, and asked where he went to medical school, which he declined to answer. I could barely understand him yet his voice seemed so familiar to me. I asked my friend Ajay in Johannesburg to try to look up the hospital. She couldn't find it either. I didn't say a word to Dean about my detective work. He left me a voice message and he really did seem quite distraught. His voice was shaky, as a person in great deal of discomfort would sound. He was either in pain, or he was a candidate for the academy award for best actor of the year.

Three days had gone by and I made the decision to send the money to pay for Dean's surgery. I listened to his message over and over again. The thought of not helping a loved one in pain was more than I could bear. I'd rather be wrong with my intuition than to feel responsible for someone to die needlessly. Those men had sought revenge on my poor Dean, and now he was laid up in hospital.

I was given an address for the translator and informed Dean the money would be sent out the following morning and should arrive at the man's house within hours. I decided to look online to locate the translator, whom I found immediately. Is it a coincidence that the person I found with the same name also happened to be an architect? Then I recalled earlier on the trip that Dean spoke about his translator being a friend, who was also an architect.

Sent from my iphone

On April 2 2013 at 5:10 PM **Michael Simon** <Michaelkind10@yahoo.co.uk> wrote:

I'm happy to hear both side now is my duty to solve this problem. Mom you want to allow this problem to destroy beautiful love? The answer is NO, I know my dad very well he's very stubborn man but he is not what you think he is angry because you involve third party anyway

Mom you build this love. You bring this family together never give up on him at least give him benefit of doubt do what you've to do to bring your husband home I know you can do this you are a strong and positive woman, I apologize on behave of him please forgive him for God sake may God bless our family

I love you mom

From: **Jane Hollis** <janehollis17@gmail.com>
To: **Michael Simon** <Michaelkind10@yahoo.co.uk>
Sent: Tuesday 2 April 2013 9.15
Subject: Re

Michael I love your father and I always will. Maybe you will understand better than he. I have never met or seen your father. He needs money and I would never fail to send it.

Understand this Michael, I'm not a wealthy woman. I have retirement put away that is in a trust. The trusts consists of four people. I can't have the money that easily. I have to show cause. My attorney wants information regarding the address to send money, and for my protection. You father lied to me about something and I can prove it. Maybe he had his reasons. He refuses to do anything to reconcile this problem. I need to know more and all he can say is I don't trust him. I gave him my heart. I trusted him with that. He said he never wanted to hear from me again, so I'm doing as he asked. I would rather die alone than to always live the way I am now. I will always love him Michael that is certain, but he no longer feels the same. For him it is over easily, for me though, my certain death will be soon. I have no more medication for blood pressure.

I love you Michael

From: **Michael Simon** Michaelkind10@yahoo.co.uk
Subject: Re
Date: April 3 2013 9.30 AM
To: **Jane Hollis** janehollis17@gmail.com

Good morning mom how was your night? I hope your husband is doing okay? Mom this is your happiness let it go do whatever its take to bring your joy home don't listen to anyone please because the money will never buy you happiness mom.

If I were you mom I will do whatever without anyone consent to provide whatever they need over there for the sake of love you have for him and order him immediately after the surgery to come home. Please you hold this family together don't allow this union to tear apart, this is my opinion mom I don't know how you feel.

I love you mom.

From: **Jane Hollis** janehollis17@gmail.com
To: **Michael Simon** Michaelkind10@yahoo.co.uk
Sent: 2 April 2013 15:07
Subject:

Michael he is not responding on Facebook. Until he does I will wait even if it takes a lifetime. Michael please ask him to open his heart or it may be too late. I'm not eating, I'm not drinking water and I haven't taken my blood pressure medicine. My life will be over without him Michael. I can't take the pain of losing him.

I love you.

Sent from my iphone

From: **Jane Hollis** janehollis17@gmail.com
Subject: Re
Date: April 3 2013 10:02 AM
To: **Michael Simon** Michaelkind10@yahoo.co.uk

Michael the whole problem is legal. I cannot change the process. I have a living trust and all monies have to be approved by 4 people. I isn't even in my control. This is the way it was set up years ago. If everyone gets angry at me because of this then so be it.. I am not able to do anything. It was made this way to protect me. My attorney will never release money without investigating the reason. This is why everyone is upset at me. If I write checks I have to give them statements each month. If I go over the allotted amount it gets deducted from the next month's allowance. That's the way it is. I had to make this request to the attorney and I won't lie to him. In time he will let me know what to do.

Your father and I have apologized to each other but there hasn't been much said since because of the hours difference.

In the past I have given away money to the poor. Now I have this trust because my children argue that I'm going to be poor, so they decided it's best that I get this under some kind of control. If your father gets angry at me for this, then maybe we are not together for the right reasons. I have always been one that prepared for every scenario that life dishes out, but this is not what I expected to happen. I never expected any of these strange turn of events. Why is he in this position? Did he not obtain health insurance?I don't know about South Africa, but hospitals here will never turn patients away. They have to be treated. The doctors take the Hippocratic oath to take care of their patients.

Adebayo Adebote, aka Ade Ade

Another translator for Dean Simon. This person started contacting Jane claiming he had also accompanied Dean to the hospital and was very concerned. He urged Jane to send more money, as outlined in the following conversations:

April 19, 2013, at 6:30 AM, Ade Ade
ade42212@gmail.com **wrote:**
Good Morning Mrs Simon I'm your husband personal translator, I just
want to let you know your husband was taking to hospital 5:30 AM this
morning his hand is swelling up and the hand has already affect his health
but I promise he will be alright.

On, April 20, 2013 at 4:19 AM, Ade Ade
ade42212@gmail.com **wrote:**
Good morning madam, I'm sorry about what happened to your husband
crime rate in my county is just too high recently I lost my wife in a clash
between police and mine workers its was deadly clash that's my story
madam. The hospital told me this morning we need to pay for the
surgery before they can do anything please any assistance you can for
him please do it we can't afford to loose him because of money no
amount of money can buy his life please once again help him I'm begging
for God sake. Mr Dean is a very positive man and strong he Love you so
much I can't describe the kind of love this man have you, don't let this
situation destroy your love.

April 20, 2013 at 7:47 AM, Jane Hollis wrote
Good Morning Ade Ade,
Dean wants me to ask you to check with the hospital regarding what is
needed. I'm not definite on what he means by what is needed, but
perhaps you can ask him. He will then let me know.
Thank you,

April 21, 2013, Jane Hollis wrote
Ade, I need to have the name of the hospital and a person I can't directly
to take care of this. Can you get me the information?

On, April 21, 2013 at 4:38 PM, Ade Ade
ade42212@gmail.com **wrote:**
I think I will sleep around here because I can't leave him for long, he was
beaten by those guys and rob him, this is the time you need to stand with
your husband.

On, April 22, 2013 at 7:45 AM, Ade Ade
ade42212@gmail.com **wrote:**
Good to hear from you, Mr. Dean will get better soon he keep asking me
did you contact my wife yet your husband truly love you. The doctor
said he might need the surgery on his hand I will let you know whatever
they need.

On April 23, 2013 at 4:08 AM, Jane Hollis wrote:
Please keep me informed. I'm terrified getting this news. Please tell him
I love him more than my life. If anything happens to him, my life is over.
Please tell him I am praying for him. Thank you for letting me know. I
feel so helpless at this great distance.

On April 23, 2013 at 9:48 AM, Jane Hollis wrote:
Good Afternoon,
I must apologize. Now that I am over the shock of my husband being in
the hospital, I'm a little calmer. Worried yes, but calmer. Could you
please tell me about his condition. I have lost contact with him. I am
terribly worried. Thank you for being our liaison in this horrible
situation.

On April 24, 2013 at 11:43 AM, Jane Hollis wrote:
I'm here for him and very worried. Please tell him I love him very much
and I'm praying for him.
Thank you.

On, April 24, 2013 at 7:45 PM, Ade Ade
ade42212@gmail.com **wrote:**
I'm trying my best here and I promise to do everything in my power to
help him because good man like your husband doesn't deserve this
situation. Mrs Simon you need to help your husband he truly love you he
can't do anything without mention your name.

May 10, 2013

The surgery apparently went well and Dean would remain in the hospital for several days. He's not going back to the project and is finally going to make plans to come home. His fare home is going to cost $6,500.00 in total. He has no money, no wallet, no computer, no employment, and now he has no place to live. I have to find a way to help him in his hour of need. He has become my responsibility because he has called me his wife and he is serious about our relationship. I told Dean there was nothing in the world I wouldn't do for him, short of breaking the law.

Dean's friend Ajeniya has been very helpful throughout all this turmoil. He has moved his two boys out of their bedroom and into their little sister's room so that Dean will have a place to stay at his modest home. Ajeniya is also a widower. His wife died in a skirmish with police when a bomb went off and she was found in a field. He sent me a link to the article, but her name wasn't actually listed among the dead.

May 17, 2013

I've been asked to send the money to Ajeniya's bank account. I have to make two deposits because I just can't get that sum of money all at once. It will take some time to get the full amount requested.

June 17, 2013

The second payment is on its way. I didn't know if it was received or not, so I need to know if Dean had gotten the money. Its several days before he contacts me and meanwhile, my imagination runs riot and I have visions of wild parties with lots of drugs and alcohol, and the fear that I had been duped. I've always been something of a clairvoyant, so now I start to wonder whether I'm doing the right thing and I'm beginning to doubt my own judgement. Eventually Dean tells that there has been a slight problem and he had been afraid to tell me the news that Ajeniya had taken a thousand dollars from the money I had sent to buy clothes and food for his family..... so Dean now needs another thousand to come home. I'm not only angry because he didn't ask permission, but now we have another delay.

June 30, 2013

This unforeseen shortfall of a thousand dollars has now been sent so that Dean could buy his airline ticket and finally come home. I'm so excited that now, at last, I can go shopping for something special to wear when Dean gets home.

When Dean next called he tells me that his ex wife had called him and asked to see Michael, and that she was living in Canada. He'd told me at the start of our relationship that she had died from cancer. I called him out on the lie, and his explanation was that he had pretended that she was out of his life and dead because she cheated, and he still felt bitter about it. He claimed to have tried to tell me this once before but I hadn't paid any attention. He's telling this to the wrong person, because I forget nothing. He later apologized, but once again, I felt as though I was speaking to a different person. During the evenings and through the night Dean was agitated and snappy, and would say hurtful things to me, but at other times he was sweet and in seemingly good spirits. When I pointed this out to him, he became very belligerent and not at all like the charming and thoughtful man that I had grown to love. The entire summer reeked havoc on my nerves. I was on medication for stress and my emotions were running wild. While trying to cope with all of Dean's problems, I lost my best friend to cancer.

July, 2013

My suspicions now are at an all time high. Dean tells me that he is very hungry and I asked why, because he was living at his translator's house and is supposedly being well looked after. I also questioned why he needed a translator when he seemed to be reasonably fluent in the local language. I'd also noticed that some of his E-mails were written under the name Edvin Dean Simon. He told me this was his birth name, which doesn't sound very Swedish to me.

Jane recalls: While getting to know each other, we spoke about past relationships. Aside from Michael's mother leaving Dean for another man, Dean met a woman that was very good to him and would do anything for him. She was from Brazil. On June 1, 2009 she departed from Rio de Janeiro to fly to France. The Air France Airbus crashed killing 228 passengers and crew members. She was supposedly one of the passengers. In 2011 he had another unsuccessful relationship. He claimed he had to be hospitalized for two weeks due to heart failure. He then said if I left him he would surely die.

WELCOME HOME

I have the house cleaned and ready for Dean's homecoming. For the entire time that Dean had been in South Africa, I'd promised him he would have a huge feast prepared for his return.

July 4, 2013

Dean called to say he ran into a problem today. The rental company for the machine that was broken said they want money to replace it and they wanted it done immediately. If only we could have gotten him out of Africa sooner they would never have located him. Now with the holiday, there is yet another delay. Dean made an appointment to speak to someone at the shop he rented the machine from. He feels certain he can negotiate a settlement.

July 10, 2013

After much negotiation and bargaining, Dean managed to calm them down at the rental company. He told me they wanted to press charges and seize his passport, and do whatever they could to get paid. I really didn't see how they could do that unless there was a court order detaining him there. They wanted their money. The machine was brand new and valued at $35,000.00. I asked why the company didn't pay the damages and he reminded me that he was subcontracting. My heart sank and all I could do was cry, be sick, and cry some more. Piece by piece and inch by inch my tired heart was breaking a little more each day. He sent me a photo of the likeness of the machine he was to replace. He also sent me a photo of the broken machinery. He said the repairs would be equal to a new one. I checked online and yes, he was on target as far as pricing is concerned. How much more financial delay would I be subject to before everything had been dealt with?

July 20, 2013

Dear Jane,

You have overcome many obstacles within your life which have made you the wonderful person you are today. You should be very proud that you have persevered all your experiences and with it you have lived, acknowledged, and learned and you have never a intentionally done unto others as it has been done unto you for you know what it feels like and you have the strength to rise above it all. You are attractive, generous, honest, humorous, intelligent, kind, lovable, loving, passionate, and a wonderful mother. May God Bless you and always give you the strength for you to continue to grow and love. I promise I will never stop loving you.
Love Always,
Your husband

July 28, 2013

I know we haven't been chatting with each other that much lately and you are doubting my ability to keep our relationship together. I want you to know that I love you so much and I will be there whenever you need me. Our love will always keep growing for each other day by day. I love you with all my heart and just know that I will always be faithful because I am yours and no one else's. No one could ever give me what you and I share because our love is unique. Even though we are far away from each other I just want you to know I will never stop loving you and we have so many things to do in our lives. I want us to do them together. I love you Jane, and I will be yours forever.

Love always,

Dean

Sent from my iPad

Above: Whenever Jane started to doubt Dean's sincerity, he would send messages like these in an effort to keep Jane hooked on the romance, and to protect his steady supply of revenue....courtesy of Jane's life savings.

*Machine similar to the one damaged by Dean's "employee" which Dean
claimed would cost $35,000 to replace*

July 30 2013
I had by now sold many things of value including my wedding ring, family
jewelery, electronics, furniture, photos, paintings and much more. I worked
endless hours these past five months, to save all I could. I did without any
small luxuries and was barely able to afford food. Sometimes I didn't have
anything to eat at all. Deep in my heart of hearts, I know this may seem like
craziness and stupidity on my part. I'm an intelligent woman and I wonder
how it is I'm in this mess. Part of me believes in Dean and feels he is being
truthful about everything and part of me has doubts. I have no way of
knowing. If I don't give him help, he could die there in that unforgiving part
of the world. If he is lying, my heart will break. No matter which way I
turn, I'm the loser. I've come this far and I feel there is no turning back.
I've already sent so much money and now I have to send more. One deposit
will go to a business account of a trusted friend. I question the likelihood
that Dean would see the money. He assured me the money will be safe in
his friend's hands. I have not heard if the money has gotten to Dean and it
should have arrived by the following day. I feel tremendous anxiety and
fear, wishing he would call me, or at the very least text me.

It's now been two days since the money was deposited, according to my bank. The bank has been very suspicious regarding my bank transfers lately. They said there were too many of them made and the location is difficult to deal with due to scammers.

Dean finally confesses he has been afraid to contact me because he knows I'll be very angry. $16,000.00 was removed to pay back taxes by the company whose account I was using for a deposit. Where do I find another large amount of cash? I sold my life insurance policy to get more money to make up for the money used. At least for now I am able to buy food. I'm driven to get Dean out of hell.

Dean and I tend to argue more and more each day. Sometimes I feel as though I'm talking to two different people…again. He never answers his phone and he is hardly texting me these days. I sleep more and more and my doctor still has me on anti depressants. Although there are no visible effects from the medicine, I feel as though my mind has slowed down and I no longer think things through or over-react. I feel numb and emotionless. I'm unbelievably tired. Dean asked me to promise I would never leave him, reminding me of all our promises we've made to each other. He makes me feel guilty if I feel doubtful. He has worked twice as hard to send me poetry, which is what he does a lot, just before he asks me to send him money. After he receives it, he fails to write for a few days. I love him more because he pours his heart out to me when he sends the poems.

Sometimes we argue in the middle of the night, which are his days due to the time difference. The lack of sleep is breaking me down. Then he gets really upset because I'm awake all the time. I can't win. His personality changes differ from night and day. He is mellow and sweet during the day and at night he becomes verbally abusive and hateful. I wonder if he is drinking, or worse, doing drugs. He blames stress. He's taken care of. Why should he be the one to be stressed?

I've learned that his translator has met a new lady and spends a lot of time and money having parties at her house. He's in love and wants to marry her, but she doesn't want his children. Ajeniya has deserted them for the love of this woman. Who gives up their children this way? I never understood that way of thinking. Ajeniya has given Dean full responsibility of taking care of the children, Joseph, John and Betty. He teaches them at home, feeds them, and sometimes there is no food. On the downside to taking care of the children there is the cost of healthcare, rent and dental bills. Dean had to take Betty to emergency for a high fever. Dean had a tooth needing to be pulled for a cost of $900.00. These things are all subtracted from the money I sent, meaning once again, it had to be replaced. Dean assured me he would be bringing the children to the U.S. to live and would I please prepare for this by locating a good school or I could home school if I wanted to do that instead.

December 15, 2013
We finally catch our first break. Dean said the company he worked for came through with the payment for his part of the work that was completed. He was so excited and said we can finally have all we've dreamed of having. I reminded him that all I ever wanted was him. He was to receive $850,000.00 …. half of which would arrive within the week and the remainder would arrive by March. The money would be sent to me and I must deposit it into my personal checking account to keep until he gets home. Already I decided it would go into a brand new account at a different bank all together.

Since it is mid winter I needed to purchase warm clothing because of course, this is a drastic climate change for the children. I deemed it time to work on the bedrooms to make them look warm and welcoming. I would try to give them a feel of Africa so it would help with homesickness they may be dealing with. I've gotten some toys and wrapped them up so they could open them on their first night home. Then something crossed my mind to add to the confusion once again. I distinctly recall Dean telling me that he had an inheritance coming to him from his father's insurance money when he turned 60. It was $850,000.00 and I feel compelled to ask, "How many times in one's lifetime, can you receive that exact same amount of money?"
Dean tells me that him and the children will be home for Christmas. I asked to speak to the children so they could get to know me before meeting me for the first time. He got angry and reminded me that they were not babies and would be fine. He seemed to forget their ages from our last discussion. In a conversation with Ajeniya during Dean's hospital care, he stated that he had two children, not three.

From Jane's diary:

January 2014

It has been 13 months since Dean and I met and I'm so intertwined with him and so close to him that I can't get through another day without him. For the first time since we've met, I want this pain to end. I'm thinking of this constant pain of loss. He makes promises and never keeps them. He's going to be coming home then he never does. I'm so tired and so sad every day and every night. Ever since I was a child, I suffered losses. My grandparents died when I was little, the only parents I had ever known. My father deserted me at birth, my mother never really wanted me. My step sisters and step brother didn't include me in their lives. My first love was killed and my husband is dead. "How much more, Lord?"

This is the day I've decided to talk to Dean about what I am feeling. I want him home and I am not ready to take "no" for an answer. This is the end of the line. If I have to live one more day without him, I would do something to end my life soon. I trust no one enough to talk about this. I can't go back to my old life before Dean. That is not an option. How can I love someone so deeply and we've never met? What is wrong with me? Every man I look at, I see Dean.

I sent a text message to Dean and I let him know I wanted to end my life and I couldn't do this any more. I have faded away from all the people I know and I want to sleep and never wake up. I am tired of the emotional upheaval.

Dean is confusing me with his mixture of anger and worry. He told me we had so much to look forward to because after all, we are still young enough to enjoy a life together. He makes everything sound so real. I want to believe him. He is my life, my love. He is my lover, my best friend, my heart, my mind and my soul. I would see him in my dreams and I sometimes sense he is near me. I could feel the warmth of his breath. I question my sanity more often.

Dean always gives me a lecture about health being wealth and how I must take care of it. He always tells me I have to be strong and not throw away true love. I have never given my answer to that statement. Part of me wanted to say, "True love would be reason to move heaven and earth to be together.. True love doesn't rely on widows to survive. True love finds work to make the money you need to come home.

I've never known anyone so attentive. Dean knows me better than I know myself. Why was he put in my path and yet I know deep down we are never going to meet? Life can be so unfair.

Sleep please take me to Dean tonight.

The man on the right is Ajeniya Afolabi. He now uses the name Afolabi Ajeniya on Facebook. The original profile shows him as an architect. That information was taken off his profile and his name was reversed. He acted as a mule for money deposits and transfers

"Ajeniya's children". Allegedly dumped on Dean after Ajeniya found love with a woman who had no interest in them.

LET'S BUY SOME CHILDREN

January 28, 2014

The children's bedrooms are finished. They're painted bright colors that would remind you of the sun on Africa. I filled them with things children love. There are three new bikes waiting for them and gifts are wrapped and placed on their beds. Dean said the children's father wants a gift from us because after all, he is giving us three children. I would have thought it would be the other way around. We are the ones deserving of a gift. Now I need $13,000.00 for the tickets to get these children home. Their father Ajeniya has no money and I should have known he wouldn't have. This time I have to take out a loan. Before I do that, I ask Dean if I could use part of the money from the check that will be sent to me from the insurance company. He now finds out the check will be sent to him in his name and will be delivered to him in South Africa….. not to me. He will make the deposit and give me all the money back that I sent him. I should have known there was no point in asking him if I could buy the children's tickets with it.

February 6, 2014

I received the loan and sent the money for the flight tickets. I haven't purchased a gift for Daddy dearest and his girl friend. They want iPhones, very expensive new cell phones, in exchange for the children. I ruled out the laptops due to the cost of shipping. They disgust me. This isn't top of my priority list at the moment. I've been sending additional money all along to feed Dean and the children. There is no work for him, the children have no one to watch them and Dean is always in pain with his shoulder and arm. I've also helped with the rent. I'm stalling now and will continue to do so for as long as I can.

< Back   Dean Simon   📞 ⓘ

I'm looking at the iPhone 6 plus gold and the iPad Air 2

The iPad Air 2 wifi+cellular is 628

Yes I know that's what you want me to send you

iPhone 6 plus gold color is 749

I'm just check it at their site

Above: One of the many phone texts sent to Jane as the demands for expensive phones and requests for more money kept coming

February 15, 2014

There is no sign of the money yet. Dean has to attend classes because he is not going to be able to take the children out of the country until they are adopted by him. He is filling out paperwork, and being interviewed by a woman at the adoption agency. She has interviewed me over the phone several times. Sometimes she gets a bit impatient because she randomly calls without notice and I don't always answer. She can't understand that I may be away from the phone or driving. I felt it was quite strange that she never asked me my qualifications for raising children or my past experience with children.

After several calls, she tells me the children's natural father is asking for two phones and $30,000.00. She recommends I give him the money or he may not give us the children and he would be greatly insulted. I almost told her that I was the one that felt insulted, but I thought better of it. I broke down and told her I can't do this anymore. I was sobbing and I remember her saying, "Don't cry. Please don't cry." She said she had a little boy and knew what I was feeling. She had no idea what I was feeling. She kept saying Dean needed me. I was simply done. I won't say anything to Dean. I need to know where this will lead me. I had a feeling this woman may have been his lover who was also in on the scam.

Don't say that

I'm just trying to think of what to do

Turning against each other just makes matters worse. Goodnight Dean. I need sleep now. I will be here when you can talk.

 I'm not fighting you okay

Ok

I just don't know what to do or say anymore.

 I've told you get this money from somewhere or someone I will sort everything out when I get home but you don't want to listen to me.

I can't borrow money. I've told you and you are not listening. Where can I go? I have one bank loan and I can't get another. Who has twenty thousand dollars? I can't take it from my retirement because they allow only one large amount a year. I've already done that.

always say in Gods time I shall have you.

I love you Dean. I'm hopelessly and helplessly in love with you.

 We need to get this money I want to go home

I want you home. I want you with me in my arms, in my life and in my bed.

Home is where your heart is and where the love is.

 They bring the money to 20 thousand with a 2 gift from us

What kind of gift? Phones?

 I don't know yet

Ok let me know

 The lady told them they're going to sign some documents before she handover their demand to them

That's a good idea

 She didn't want them to demand for anything again

They may try

People get stupid when they get greedy

She told she's going to airport with us
the we're leaving

 Day

Ok

 She said she's not going to allow
anyone to disturb us

I am glad she is along the effort to help
you at the airport.

I will try my best

He and his girlfriend complain to the
lady we refuse to give them gift when
they ask and I told the lady the guy
spend the money my wife sent to me

 I was angry, sad and crying today

Yes he did take money from you. He's a
barbarian and should not have the
children at all

 We're taking them away my wife

I want to love them. I want to give them
happiness.

I just go days not able to eat.

I seem to be existing but not really living.

 Then you're not helping us

Dean I have a very sensitive stomach. If I go through anxiety I get sick. I did it today. I told you this a long time ago.

It's not something I do on purpose. It's my nature. I've been this way all my life.

I even had many tests done to find the problem and there was none. I just have to remain calm as much as possible.

 We need to be home soon

Yes I know

Can you use the money

That you will be getting

 I can only cash the check when I get home there's no other way

I see

 I will pay off everything when I get home

February 25, 2014

In today's mail I received the much desired check that will take me out of debt and put our lives together. I'm so happy, beyond belief. At last we are free of all this pain and suffering we've endured for so long. But…I can't believe what I'm seeing! The check was made out to me, but the amount was incorrect. Instead of $425,000.00, half of total of $850,000,00, the amount was for $4,500.00. I photographed it and sent it to Dean. He was angry, not only because of the check not being made out to him, but for the incorrect amount as well. He has called the Insurance Company to rectify the problem and they in turn deposited the correct amount to his bank account.

I looked at the return address label and spotted a PO Box number for a city in Utah. Could Dean actually be in Utah? His name was on the return address. This so-called Insurance Company was located in a town only 30 minutes away from where I live. I looked online and discovered an electronics company with the same name. What does this company have to do with Dean? He had said the balance of his payout would come to us after he gets back to the states. By now I was totally confused.

As I was browsing through Facebook, something took me by complete surprise. There was Dean, but with a different name. The man I was looking at called himself Danie Van Jaarsveld. I looked through his profile and focused my attention on the photos of his family members. I learned this man had two sons, not one. Michael was actually Ettienne and the other son, whom I had never seen before, was Jean-Pierre. Dean said he had no family apart from his son. Danie Van Jaarsveld has a sister. Danie worked for SBM Offshore and Dean for Simon Ventures. I decided to log on to LinkedIn. Dean was no longer Dean on LinkedIn. He was now Danie, and Simon Ventures is now non-existent. It is now SBM Offshore from Whitbank in Africa. I saved every photo this man had on his site. I copied family names and researched each of their profiles. I read that Danie was in a relationship with a girl, much younger, by the name of **Nathasia Michelle Rost** who was around half his age. She had a baby girl and I wondered if the baby was Dean's or Danie's. Was this put into play by my Dean or was Danie the legitimate man in the photo? I'm sick inside but I'm no longer weak. I'm angry. I want answers, and I want them now.

March 1, 2014

I just asked Dean to send me a photo of him with today's date written on a piece of paper. I told him he had placed doubt in my mind. I never asked him about the return address on the envelope and I never mentioned my discovery regarding the electronics company. These things I kept to myself for now. Even though Dean was furious with me, my request was honored and a photo was sent to my E-mail address that same night. He asked if I was pleased with the photo and I got the usual lecture about true love and trust. I told him I was pleased, and I was, until I looked a bit closer. The pose was an identical one to a photo on Danie Van Jaarsveld's profile. His jacket was painted green over the original tan, and the note bearing his name was whitened over the top of a painting he was holding. It was in script writing and the whole thing looked like it had been photo-shopped.

When I confronted Dean he was not at all angry, which I assumed was because he had no way out of this one. He said he was ready to tell me the truth. I couldn't help but wonder if he really knew the truth if it hit him in the face. He confessed he was only 40 years old and he was afraid I would not care for a younger man. That was why he hid behind the photo of a man my own age. I was up a notch on being heartbroken. I felt deceived and part of me died that day. For a very long time, it was the older version of Dean Simon that I held close to my heart, and now I had to try to figure out what was really going on. I told him I needed time to think about it and he told me that he understood. I had to see where all this would lead, what might happen next, and what the final outcome would be. I knew that from that day I broke down on the phone to the "adoption agent," that I wouldn't part with a single dime more. I had nothing left to give. That part was behind me for certain. I was no longer the goose that laid the golden egg.

The heart wants what the heart wants. I want to find this other man, and one day I would, but all I know was that I fell in love with the man that I had shared my heart and soul with. I wasn't ready to give him up just yet. I still believed he had children that needed a mother. I'd committed myself to a life with Dean. I was willing to take a chance, yet I still needed answers. I needed to find out the truth about everything.

I tried to find answers through the internet. I spent endless hours searching dating sites and different scam sites. I found a letter of a complaint about a man asking for money on a dating site, and there was a photo of a man named Simon Dean. In the photo was Dean Simon, getting into a car and smoking a cigarette. My Dean said he didn't smoke. This is now the second photo of him smoking a cigarette that I have seen.

Dean began to sense that I was pulling away from him, and I now exercised extreme caution. Who had I really been talking to all this time? I realized that I really had no idea at all. Dean became jealous and insulting. I have to tear myself away from him or he will destroy me. The reality has dawned on me that I had been taken for a ride. I really can't explain the hurt and the anguish. My finances are in tatters and I refuse to send him anything more. I stopped taking most of his calls and I tried to keep busy with as many activities as I possibly could. Without distractions I would fall to pieces. How do I break away from someone I thought I loved so much? It hurts more than anything I have ever known before. It's a terrifying feeling knowing deep down that you have been well and truly duped, even though there is still a small part of you that wants to believe that it's not happening. Then came the anger and the resentment, and the need for justice. Time for detective Jane Hollis to step forward.

After searching through several dating sites and anti-scam sites on an almost daily basis, I finally found Dean, or to be more precise….multiple profiles of Dean. According to the dates on some of the dating sites, he had been listed on them for the entire time that he was trying to convince me that I was the love of his life. He used a variety of different names that had been flagged as scammer profiles. My heart sank just a little bit further.

There was **Patrick Roeder**, seeking women 18-99. How about **Alex Owalabi**? Alex is a black African that uses the stolen photos of white men, including the younger versions of the Dean Simon photos. Then there's **Lampart Roselenee**, who claims to be straight, with other entries declaring him to be bisexual. These and other profiles are using the very same photos of Dean, though the names frequently change.

I can't argue with Dean anymore. I feel shattered. I don't want to argue about anything anymore. I'm tired and I feel empty. It's Halloween night and there is no more appropriate time than now to end this charade. There is only one way to end it and make everything final, and that's to try and play him at his own game.

I send a text to Dean pretending to be one of my children. He will be afraid to talk to my sons. He would never stand up to Jimmy, especially after he always remembered my sons and I would come after him if he approached any of the children on my friend's list. My son Jimmy told Dean that I passed away this morning due to a heart attack. Dean replied that he had therefore lost his best friend and he asked Jim to please fulfil his mother's wishes for him to come home with the children, and could he please send him the money. My son assured him that he would do everything that was asked of him. Dean was to inherit everything I had, but he was to collect his inheritance by coming to the U.S. to claim it. Information was given to Jimmy as to where the money should be sent for Dean to come home. Of course the money was never sent, so it never arrived. Stalling for time, Dean was told that someone else may have collected the money. My son let him beg all through the holidays, and he continued to communicate for another three months. Not once did Dean appear to show any kind of genuine remorse at the news of my "death". It was of course, far more important to insist that more money was sent to cover the cost of travel for Dean and the three bogus children supposedly under his care.

Dean Simon

CEO at Simon Ventures

Location
　　　Hartford, Connecticut
Industry
　　　Architecture & Planning

Current　　　1. Simon Ventures

Previous　　　1. Coca Cola Sweden

Education　　1. St. Bridget of Sweden School, Vancouver Island University

17 connections

Join LinkedIn and access Dean's full profile. It's free!

As a LinkedIn member, you'll join 400 million other professionals who are sharing connections, ideas, and opportunities.

- See who you know in common
- Get introduced
- Contact **Dean** directly

View Dean's Full Profile

Experience

- Architect

  Simon Ventures

  May 1994 – Present (22 years 2 months)

- Architecture & Planinig

  Simon Ventures

  May 1994 – Present (22 years 2 months)

Architecture & Planning

- CEO

  Simon Ventures

  May 1994 – Present (22 years 2 months)

  We construction industry designing new buildings, restoring and conserving old buildings and developing new ways of using existing buildings. We are involved in construction projects from the earliest stages right through to completion..our work include:
  preparing and presenting design proposals to clients
  advising clients
  producing detailed drawings
  negotiating with contractors and other professionals
  attending regular meetings with clients, contractors and other specialists
  co-ordinating the work of contractors
  making site visits to check on progress
  dealing with problems that might come up during building.

- Production manager

  Coca Cola Sweden

  September 1981 – August 1993 (12 years)

Languages

- **English**
- **Swedish**

Education

- **St. Bridget of Sweden School, Vancouver Island University**

  Bachelor of Architecture, Architecture

  1977 – 1980

Groups

-

  Revit Users

Above: One of Dean Simon's several profiles. This one is from Linkedin

I want you home with me

 My wife

 Are you okay?

 Please talk to me

 Jane where are you

 Please talk to me

Mr Simon I have my mother's cell. I'm trying to contact all her friends. I regret to inform
you my mother passed away at 3 am. She wrote you an email and ask that I send it upon her death. She's going to be sadly missed. I'm sorry.

 Oh my God

I'm sad

Where's she?

She had another stroke. Mr. Simon I can't tell you how distressed my family is at this time. She kept us together. She wanted me to tell you she loved you and tried to be strong and do what was right. She asked that we not publish things and keep it private. So I have to make calls for a private and small funeral. Thank you for making her happy when no one else could. I would have wished her happiness but none of us could do what you could for her.

 This is so sad for me

She asked to be cremated. The funeral home picked her up.

I love her so much

My life is empty without her

Mr. Simon I had nearly forgotten, she asked that her ashes be sent to South Africa to you. Think about it and let me know what you decide. Yes I know how you feel. I can't begin to tell you.

I don't know what to say

 She was my best friend

She knew she was dying and didn't want you to know.

More than anything she wanted you here.

My mother made bedrooms for your kids. She had toys and books ready for them. It was all unexpected. If you ever come to the U.S. I would like it if you stayed at her house. You would get a sense of what love she put into everything.

I'm in serious pain

 Jane is gone I'm finish

We're all suffering today. You have to go on. We all do. It's what she would want you to do.

 I can't go on without my love

You have to.

 I can't

I can't

Is there someone you can talk to about it. Give this time. It will take a lot of time.

You will heal.

 I can't heal

Do you have a priest

She said you were catholic

 Yes

Then talk to him.

My mother left you a beautiful letter she sent to your Email.

 He can't replace my love

You can contact me anytime today. I don't know what to do about her phone. It will be a while before I shut it down.

Thank you

 God bless you

If there is anything I can tell you or you would like for me to do let me know. There's a lot to be done here. I'm at her house and it feels pretty empty without her.

God bless you

If there is anything I can tell you or you would like for me to do let me know. There's a lot to be done here. I'm at her house and it feels pretty empty without her.

 Okay I will

I wish you the very best. Just remember the love you shared and the time you had together. God Bless you too for looking after my best friend and Mom.

I will never stop loving her for the rest of my life

The most difficult time in your life is losing a wife or a mother. If you believe in heaven then you can believe you are going to be together again, but only if you are true to God and have faith. Live a good life my friend and you'll meet again. She was a good woman and I know she's with God now.

I know she's coming to take me soon

 I want to be with her

That may be. My great grandparents were never apart in 42 years of marriage and only stayed apart 5 months when he died. I know how much she loved you. Her eyes would smile when she smoke about you. When she was sad she would be completely different.

 I love her so much

Are you there?

Hello

How's everything?

I just want to ask you if you have my email address? Because I'm not going to come to Facebook anymore

Coming to Facebook give me bad memories

 I will forever miss my best friend, my wife

My mother has it in her address

 Okay good

I'm so sorry you feel this much sadness.

 You can contact me

Is it deansimon55@aol.com

I was thinking of taking out my mothers page, but it seems so final. I just can't do it.

 I just hope soon you'll make her dream come true by helping me and kids out

December 28, 2014

Time has passed in a daze, and my heart is still broken, and all the promises I lived for are broken promises…..broken into a million pieces. I can't forget and my reasons to carry on are gone and I can't live with the pain anymore. I contemplated ending my life on more than one occasion, only to be disrupted by the doorbell or the phone ringing. Prompted by my friend Judi I knew it was not meant for me to die, but instead, to look for closure, and to get my life back. I was once told I sometimes had an acid tongue, so I chose to put my acid tongue to work by telling my story and educating those same vulnerable and lonely people such as myself who one day, might find themselves in a similar situation to my own…. as the victim of a romance scam.

In late January 2015 I found an E-mail that was in the junk mail folder on my Google account. It was written by an attractive man about my age. I read it again. My radar was immediately alerted due to the familiarity of the contents of the letter. I'd read stuff like this before. The man's name was **Williams Dickson**, a widow from Austin Texas, age 58. He had a 9 year old daughter. We started to correspond. I was curious. However, he never wanted to talk to me on the phone, so I was suspicious that he was in fact Dean Simon…whoever Dean Simon really is….which is something I will probably never know. After I got rid of Williams, I got an email from Dean wishing me the best of luck with my new man. I was right to suspect that it was Dean in one of his various guises. I really don't care now.

Over time I received numerous suspicious friend requests, one of which was from a young girl who was much too young to fit the criteria of a woman who had been scammed. She claimed that she needed to speak to me about my experience with a scammer. My answer was, "What makes you feel that anyone here knows anything about being scammed?" I got no reply. Another one of Dean's characters? More than likely….

Jane told us: The entire time spent with Dean Simon was filled with emotion, betrayal, arguments and confusion. There was so much let down, sadness, fear, and chaos and anger. I don't know if writing about it is enough to show the array of ranging emotions. The most frustrating part of this ordeal was not being able to vent my anxieties to anyone. No one would have understood it, and I was in complete denial. I refused to believe Dean was a liar. I was brainwashed and I would not believe otherwise, even when it seemed obvious that I was being scammed.

CASH AMOUNT SENT	DATE	AMOUNT
FEDEX SHIPPING AND DUTIES		$196.44
		$361.19
		$334.21
		$143.73
WIRE FEES AND MONEY SENT		
PARTIAL LIST		
	4/21/2013	$925.00
	5/10/2013	$3,025.00
	5/17/2013	$6,500.00
	5/22/2013	$2,950.00
	6/17/2013	$6,500.00
	7/20/2013	$3,025.00
	7/31/2013	$1,500.00
	8/10/2013	$5,525.00
	8/15/2013	$13,075.00
	8/30/2013	$14,775.00
MONEYGRAM	9/12/2013	$1,520.00
	10/28/2013	$3,705.00
	12/10/2014	$1,525.00
	1/30/2014	$10,025.00
	2/10/2014	$10,025.00
	2/28/2014	$12,006.00
	7/29/2014	$1,875.00
	9/10/2014	$1,625.00
MONEY FOR CLOTHING		$1,600.00
MONEY FOR CLOTHING		$1,400.00
FOOD TOTAL IN 2 YEARS		$3,000.00
CAR CHARGER		$32.00
SAMSUNG GALAXIE S4		$1,693.75
HOSPITAL FOR BETTY		$1,739.09
ITUNES GIFT CARDS		$600.00
IPAD		$800.00
IPHONE 4S UNLOCKED		$900.00
RENT $360.00 MO. X12		$4,320.00
DENTIST FOR DEAN		$900.00
TOTAL		$118,126.41

Above: Jane's calculations on the money she sent to scammer Dean Simon during the course of their "relationship" which totalled at over $118,000

Ade422112@gmail.com   Ade Ade

deansimon55@aol.com   **Dean Simon**

michaelkind10@yahoo.co.uk Michael Simon

edvinsimon@ymail.com   Dean Simon

Places Where Money Was Sent

AMA Investment (Pty)   April 11, 2013 9:05 am
Account: 202225127
Branch: Braamfontein
Branch Code: 4805
Bank Name: Standard Bank
Swift Code: SAZAZAJJ

SBG Solutions PtyLtd.
Bank: First National Bank
Account: 62430796930
Branch: Braamfontein
Branch Code: 251905
Swift Code: FIRNZAJJ
IBAN Code: 250655

Alvin Kadwell (found on Facebook) 5-20-14 3:14 pm
513 South State St.
Big Rapids, MI 49307
Bank: Fifth and Third Bank
Savings Acct: 9903879139
Address: 101 N. Michigan Ave. Big Rapids, MI 49307
Routing: 072401404
Bank Phone: 231-592-4100
Swift Code: FTBCUS3C
He may later have changed routing number due to incorrect information given from
where he signed up for an account opening.

Alvin Kadwell
513 South State St.

Routing: 072401404
Bank Phone: 231-592-4100
Swift Code: FTBCUS3C
He may later have changed routing number due to incorrect information given from
where he signed up for an account opening.

Alvin Kadwell
513 South State St.
Big Rapids, MI 49307
Bank Name: Lake Oseola State Bank
Bank Address: 790 North Michigan Ave., Baldwin, MI 49307
Bank Phone: 231-745-4601
Savings Account: 5800141

New Bank:
Alvin Kadwell   5-23-14   8:57 a.m.
711 Maple St.   9-4-2014   9:07 a.m.
Big Rapids, MI 49307   9-10-14   11:46 a.m. $625.00
Bank Phone: 231-796-3516
Account: 2600757
Routing Number: 072403004

Cynthia Munson   2 found on Facebook
Bank Name: Simmesport State Bank
Bank Address: 16495 Highway 1, Simmesport, LA 71369
Accounting: 0512923
Routing: 065204951

Ann Marie Howard   sometimes goes by Marie Howard
Bank Name: Citizen Bank   works with Chinese deaf in Boston
Account: 1321257195   lives in Quincy, MA
Bank Address: 1200 Hancock St.
Quincy, MA 02169
Routing: 211070175
Bank Phone: 617-247-0782
Home Address: 52 Warren Ave. Apt. 2
Quincy, MA 02170

Accounts seem to change after each transaction I made.

Sent a package to Dean in c/o:
Gwigwi Mrwebi Street
Brickfield Complex Flat 213
New Town, Johannesburg, SA

*This is the profile photo used by **Ann Marie Howard** of Quincy, Massachusetts, USA. She claims to work with deaf Chinese people. Her brother supposedly met Dean in Cape Town, South Africa.*

*Jane said: I sent money to Ann Marie to forward to her brother, who would then give Dean the money. Also, there was **Cynthia Munson** whose sister stole $5000.00 while we were trying to find the money for back taxes. There were so many people involved that it was hard to keep track of them all.*

Jane's online digging also led her to the following conclusions as the facts regarding Dean and his many aliases' were gradually uncovered.

FACTS

The name Edvin Dean Simon is not of Swedish Origin. My paternal great grandparents were from Sweden; therefore, I have a little knowledge regarding surnames of that nationality.   When Dean told me he was from Sweden, he didn't elaborate on his background or ask me any questions.

He once said he didn't smoke, yet some photos showed that he did.

Dean "fell in love" the first week of contact.

My earlier phone calls were with a man who had a deep accent and a voice to match. I barely understood what he said. After a time he became easier to understand with a softer voice. My suspicions were that he had to get someone else to talk to me. There was always a period of waiting before we spoke. If I called him, he never answered the phone. In 2013 I obtained international calling. He would usually call me or would signify when to call him.

He said his birthday was **February 14th,** and that he was 58 years old. I thought to myself, "That's an easy date for you to remember for all the women in your life." He pretended to be living in Hartford Connecticut. He said he lived there for 12 years. Later he changed it to 12 months. I located a Dean Simon in that area. I once called the number and the woman that answered sounded a bit testy and said he no longer lived there, and she had no idea where he was. My suspicions grew following that call. However, this may be coincidental.

Ajeniya Afolabi, received money on behalf of "Dean".   I suspect he may have been the scammer using the name of Dean Simon, but I may never know.

Dean had a profile on **LinkedIn** under the guise of **Simon Ventures.** He was an architect, yet there are only women on his account and no men. I can no longer find this business online to date. The closest I've come to this name is **Simonet Ventures**, but no sight of Dean Simon.

Once he gets backed into a corner, he has a noticeable stutter.

He gets confused about the time difference between my country and his location.

Once he called me Mrs Dean instead of Mrs Simon, as though he didn't know his own last name, though there seems to be considerable use of two Christian names which are often used in reverse order, hence the confusion on the scammer's part.

Vancouver University 205-753-3245

He claims to have graduated from this university. They never heard of him.

Although he was still a citizen of Sweden, he did not want me to contact the Swedish Embassy in South Africa. He claimed he had no business contacts, personal friends, or family in Sweden.

He continually asked for cell phones.

He stated that financial assistance is a proof of true love.

He used the words "soul mate" and "destiny" frequently.

On the plus side, when I had him convinced I was hungry, he said I could take $500 out of my own money, to get food and he will take the rest. Somewhere in that scamming mentality, he had a heart. All of the paperwork from my bank showed my account number. He could have used it, but luckily for me, he didn't. However, I did change accounts not long after I realized that account numbers were visible after sending him proof of cash transfers I had sent him

He would text me in the middle of the night and those were the times I felt as though I was speaking to someone else. During the day Dean was sweet and kind, in stark contrast to evening and night calls when Dean seemed angry all the time. The angry Dean was very argumentative and verbally abusive. He continuously made remarks about me loving my money and that God won't forgive me for being selfish.

Overuse of emoticons, typical of a scammer.

If I asked questions, he would go offline a few minutes or longer, either to avoid the subject or maybe ask someone for advice for an appropriate answer

He claimed $5,000.00 was stolen from him by the sister of **Cynthia Munson,** who was another go between receiving money on Dean's behalf.

216721653546: Phone number to the adoption agency.

Poems and letters were sent to me at the times when money had been requested or recently sent.

One poem arrived as a template.

We barely spoke on Sundays

He appears to speak the native language fluently.

Dr. Stephen Muller 278 (49) 6920, refused to give me his medical education background and got irritated when I asked. Diagnosis: dislocated shoulder, separated. Internal injuries.

Samoseli Memorial Medical Hospital
hospitalsamoseli@yahoo.co.za

At the time he was taken to the hospital, he stated he had a different translator by the name of **Ade Ade**. He appears on Facebook as well as **Ajeniya** and both state they are self employed.

A certificate of deposit shows what he earned on the project he was doing in South Africa. This was coincidentally the same amount of money his father left him in an inheritance. It all indicated to me that he did not remember what he had told me previously, on any given subject.

Uses the names **Dean Simon on Facebook, Simon Edvin and Dean Simon Edvin, on My Space.** On December 10, 2013, he was reported to have used the name **Simon Edwards** in a scam. This was documented on **Romance Scams.**

Williams Dickson
williamsdick@0110outlook.com

58 years old
Suspected as being Dean Simon
Austin, TX
Originally from
Father/ Native American/mother Durango, TX
9 year old daughter
alleged DOB Feb 7
Architect
Arrived in Doha Qatar 1/27-15
Widowed
Uses romance letters
Nigerian Accent

Photo shows no sign of being Native American. He uses a typical scenario regarding his departure on an overseas job.
He has not offered to let me hear his voice by phone call.

Williams Dickson: Approached Jane shortly after she broke contact with Dean Simon. The same person is suspected to be behind both fake profiles, and that of Danie Van Jaarsveld and several more...

Jane said: Williams sent me an email a few days after "my death". It became apparent however, that Williams was probably Dean.... or vice versa. Dean sent me an e-mail congratulating me on finding a new man and wishing me all the happiness in the world. I had already suspected Williams was a scammer, and by now I was alert to suspect profiles and soon consigned him to the spam folder.

DANIE VAN JAARSVELD

I left a message for Danie to get in touch with me and after a few days there was no response. I then look at LinkedIn and when I saw his account, I left a message for him to contact me because I had information that would be of great interest to him. Within 48 hours we were messaging on Facebook Messenger. I told him everything I had suspected and he empathized with me. I informed him I located an account with his photo with the name, Dean Simon and that Dean Simon's account was used to scam me. Dean had removed his own account. Danie seemed appalled and upset with the fact I had been a victim and that his son's photo had been used as part of the scam. Before our conversation was over, he claimed he contacted Facebook and the imposter " Dean Simon" was immediately removed from Facebook. That was when I became suspicious because it seemed Facebook took Danie's word as truth rather quickly. There is usually some probing by Facebook and the offending accounts are usually suspended while awaiting I.D verification. They are rarely removed immediately.

Jane added: That's when I decided to fake my death again and move on. He never responded to my "death" and most people would have. It seems apparent that he was also a scammer. It was probably "Dean" himself.

From: Jane Hollis <janehollis17@gmail.com>
Date: December 17, 2014 at 8:11:46 AM EST
Subject: PLEASE DONT DELETE THIS UNTIL YOU'VE READ MY TEXT.

To: Danie Van Jaarsveld

PLEASE DONT DELETE THIS UNTIL YOU'VE READ MY TEXT.

I've tried to friend you on Facebook several months ago because there was something I needed to tell you. Before I begin, please understand, I mean you no harm. I want nothing but for you to read this. It will cost you nothing but a little time.

My name is Jane Hollis. I live in Ohio, USA, and you can find me on Facebook. I have been on Facebook several years and I have a closed account.

In December, 2012 I was approached by a man on Facebook that began a two year relationship that cost me a lifetime of my income and nearly cost me my life. I know you are wondering why I'm telling you this. It's simple, he was using your photos and using the fictitious name of Dean Simon. He is in South Africa, supposedly, near Johannesburg. He is also exploiting photos of you and your youngest son. I have been searching throughout the internet and found your photos under many similar yet different names. For more than a year he had me convinced he was in love with me and we would have a future together.

I asked him where he got your photo he said he found it on the internet. I couldn't help but wonder if he knew you and acquired your photos on your Facebook page.

I became suspicious when he made a mistake with one of your photos. I'm not going into detail on the things he did in error, because I have to trust you before I can divulge evidence in the event you may not be the real man in the photo on Facebook. Once I caught his error, he then changed photos and told me he was afraid I wouldn't want to meet a younger man which was his reasons for using your photo. Not that you are that old mind you, but he was only 39 supposedly. This caused a lot of confusion for me. I fell in love with two different faces but one individual man. It was difficult to comprehend. We had history, I had to stay with what I knew, I don't go from one man to another. I was in this relationship for better for worse, so I remained until I found more evidence I was being scammed.

I continued listening to his stories about him working in South Africa, and his only son getting into a bad accident, and having everything stolen after he was beaten, machinery getting damaged, having surgery from his beating, buying transportation tickets so he can come home, someone had stolen some of the money I sent him, then adopting three children. Over a hundred thousand dollars of hard earned money I sent to a scammer. The money wasn't what hurt me the most, it was the lies and deceit I could no longer live with. I contemplated suicide on more than one occasion, and I had to take medication to get me right again and still I hung on…. at least until the last request for money. He wanted me to send thirty thousand dollars to the parents of the children he was adopting. Paying for children is more than I can handle. I drew the line there. It's now over and I'm recovering. I felt compelled to tell you about this man. I have nothing to gain from it, most of all there is nothing more to lose. I simply felt I should let you become aware of your photos being misused online.

Thank you for your time. I am very sorry you have been abused also. There are cruel and evil people in the world. There are also many good people. I'd like to think I'm one of the good people. I have a kind, generous heart but I am also strong and will survive this broken heart.

I hope having your photo exploited will not cause you a future problem, but it is on a scam site which I came across by total accident. You are a victim too.

If you need proof that I'm legitimate, you can friend me on Facebook and you can view my profile and anything else on my page that may make you feel more comfortable. In twenty four hours I will unfriend you and you can go about your life. I simply felt the need to tell you about this. I just hope this man hasn't gotten other information about you that can cause you more harm.

Thank you for your time.

Jane Hollis

Sent from my iPad

.ıll AT&T 🛜   12:56 AM   33% 🔋

www.419scam.org/emails/2012-04-12/0022c285.1.htm

DateHoo... | How you... | ✕ 419 sc... | Location... | Coca-Col... | ic32009r... | LTGTBT:... | monteca... | Date.com | Search... | ≫ | +

From: "MR EDWIN SIMON" *(may be fake)*
Reply-To: <edwinsimon34@hotmail.com>
Date: Thu, 12 Apr 2012 01:50:39 -1100
Subject: Dear Friend,

Dear Friend,
Funds transfer proposal.

NOTE: Before you proceed reading this mail, this is true and not one of those mails you see on the internet, I am about to retire and here in Africa service is not
adequately rewarded I tell you the gospel truth, hence do not blame me on this, I only need you to help me so that we can smile in future, GOD bless you as you read.

I presume this mail will not be a surprise to you. I am an accountant in the mineral commission department of Ministry of Mines and Energy Ghana and also a member of contracts awarding committee of this ministry under Ghana government. I got your full information from Chamber of Commerce and industry on foreign business relations here in Accra-Ghana. And I believed you must be trustworthy and honest main looking at your profile.

Some years ago, Ghana government asked this committee to awards contracts to foreign firms, which I and my colleagues happened to be the head of this committee. With our good position, this contract was over invoiced to the tune of US$10,500,000:00 as a deal to be benefited by the two Members of this committee. Now the contracts value has been paid off to the actual contractors that executed these jobs, all we want now is a trusted foreign partner like you that we shall front with her banking account number to Claim the over inflated sum. The said funds will be shared within us when it is confirmed into your provided Account in your country by the paying Bank.

NOTE: I know there may be scams and junk mails flying here and there on the internet but certainly, this is not one. Please do not fail to understand that in spite of all that, opportunities of this kind still abound. If you have ever wished or prayed for something good to come your way, now I urge you to take this message seriously and with an open mind.

You could never know. This may be an answer to your prayers. So please give it a benefit of doubt and with good faith and trust join me and I am assuring you now that you will never be disappointed. Kindly respond back to me with your information.....Country, Mobile number, fax, Email.

God Bless you.

Mr. Edwin Simon

mail:edwinsimon34@hotmail.com

Above: Found during searches of anti-scam sites. A 419 advanced fee fraud letter generated by a Mr Edwin Simon, who is possibly also one and the same "Dean Simon" aka Williams Dixon, Danie Van Jaarsveld, and several others.

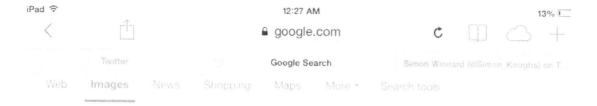

Twitter   Google Search   Simon Winnard (@Simon Keoghs) on T...

Web   Images   News   Shopping   Maps   More ▾   Search tools

100 × 100
More sizes

Results for *danie van jaarsveld*

Danie Van Jaarsveld - South Africa profiles | LinkedIn

za.linkedin.com/pub/dir/Danie/Van+Jaarsveld
80 × 80 View the profiles of professionals on LinkedIn named **Danie Van Jaarsveld** located in the South Africa. There are 5 professionals named **Danie Van Jaarsveld** in ...

Danie van Jaarsveld - South Africa | LinkedIn

za.linkedin.com/pub/danie-van-jaarsveld/32/399/110
Witbank Area, South Africa · Production Superintendent at SBM
100 × 100 Join LinkedIn and access **Danie van Jaarsveld's** full profile. It's free! As a LinkedIn member, you'll join 250 million other professionals who are sharing ...

Van jaarsveld - Witbank Area, South Africa - LinkedIn

za.linkedin.com/pub/.../za-5904-Witbank-Area.-South-Africa
80 × 80 Van jaarsveld in Witbank Area. South Africa. 20 of 20 profiles. View Full Profile · Kobus Van Jaarsveld. Title: Sales .... **Danie van Jaarsveld**. Title: Production ...

DANIE - Witbank Area, South Africa - LinkedIn

www.linkedin.com/pub/.../+/za-5904-Witbank-Area.-South-Afri...
80 × 80 There are 25 professionals named DANIE in the Witbank Area. South Africa. who use LinkedIn to exchange information. ideas. and ... **Danie van Jaarsveld**.

Dean Simon - Hartford, CT | MyLife®

www.mylife.com/simondean90
100 × 100 Are you looking for Dean Simon's contact info? Look no further. MyLife® is the one place where you can easily find and connect with people.

*Multiple accounts were discovered under the names of "Dean Simon",
"Simon Dean", and "Danie Van Jaarsveld"*

TODAY

It's been nearly two years since "my death." I made a pledge to myself to make life hell for every scammer that approaches me, and on occasion, I'll go looking for them myself. Once I do find a scammer, then I expose them on social media revealing them as the greedy sub humans they are. Who do I report them to?...enforcement agencies in the states? They themselves don't seem to be able to touch these parasites, and yet the parasites have taken their place among us. In my situation as in most cases, I also had the guy, or several others in the middle, the scammer's sidekicks, who often acts as a go between and are always on hand to try to add credibility to the scammer's stories. Call them mules, money launderers, or whatever. They often work as teams. The scammers are taking money across and within U.S and European borders, and sending it back and forth to Africa where most romance scams originate, and with the information I had to hand, I have been able to turn some of them in. Once reported, you rely on the law to do their part, but prosecutions are rare as the scammers are adept at covering their tracks. I may never know if they were prosecuted or not, but I'm getting a great deal of satisfaction from throwing myself in the mix and making the scammers source of income just that little bit harder to find.

In various on-line forums and scam support groups I try to teach people what they have to look for and have successfully stopped some lonely hearts from falling into that same pit of despair. Some will never believe they are being scammed because love is blind, and the victims are blinkered. But I won't give up trying to educate people until one day, these scammers will hopefully become past history, but in all fairness, that's an unrealistic expectation. There needs to be stronger enforcement worldwide for cyber crimes so we can be rid of these scamming low life's, who have no morals, and not one ounce of guilt shown towards the people whose lives they have torn apart.

I live on to help others in some way or another. I now have a much better grip on money and I will continue to work until I die, because it's all I have. I'm not interested any more in filling the vacancy for Mr Right, period.... because I can't feel that unconditional love for someone anymore and probably never will again. That's the sad part about it all. My trust has gone.

What I felt for Dean Simon was exhausting, yet a once in a lifetime love. I gave that relationship 120% and I have nothing left to give, or to show for it.

A part of me is still delusional with my way of thinking. I imagine finding the real man in the photo and falling in love with him all over again. Every man I see with the likeness of Dean still hurts, and sometimes his Face on LinkedIn images brings back painful memories. I must be turning the corner now though because I managed to tell parts of this story without drowning in tears. Even after all that has happened, I can't feel hate anymore towards "Dean" and I no longer have a desire to get even, because I know his place in hell is already booked, and I know he'll burn for eternity…….

My utmost thanks to the two authors, Judi and Stephen. Without their patience and understanding, my story may never have been told.

Despite Jane's torment and her feelings of despair, and the financial loss she suffered, she is determined to be part of the growing crusade to thwart romance scammers and create more awareness on the subject. She is indeed, determined to educate both victims, and potential victims by all means possible, and to offer support and advice to all those who may be in doubt about the pitfalls of hoping to find romance on-line. Jane is currently active as an influential member of an established Facebook "Scam Awareness and support group".

To gain more knowledge regarding the transfer of payments to scammers, co-author Judi Huggins contacted a bank and was granted the following interview.....

An Interview With Tiffany

I've managed to get an interview with someone working at a financial institution that transfers money to foreign countries. I had several interesting answers to questions I had for her that I would like to share with you. Her statement is as follows;

"Most of the victims range in age from 55 to 65 years of age. Why?"

Because at this age most women are well established and have easily accessible savings and retirement funds

"How do they respond to you when you deny them the transfers they are requesting?"

Most of these women will cry, knowing their scammer will be angry at them, a few become irate and frustrated, and some are grateful of the warning, and then go home to think about what they have been told.

"What is the average amount being sent?

The average is thousands of dollars and the typical victim is one with low self esteem, widowed, and/or down on their luck.

"Do you see a frequent trend with regard to the monies being transferred out of the US?" Also, where do the victims send money to?

Payments are infrequent but not uncommon. However, what is being sent usually goes to Ghana and Nigeria, which are the scamming hot spots.

"Is there a specific ethnic group being targeted for a romance scam?"

The most frequent victim is Caucasian.

"Have you had formal training with regard to scammers?"

Yes, we have had extensive training and we are able to detect a scam immediately. Other facilities like ours are rather passive about this problem and seem to be overlooking the signs. We are very concerned about this epidemic. In all sincerity, the best solution to the problem would be to educate as many people as possible.

"How do you make the initial discovery that the person sending money is being scammed?"

We ask questions. Are you sure you know this person? Is this person related to you? Have you ever seen him/her? What is the reason for sending this money?

Tracee Douglas

Tracee Douglas is from Bundaberg, Queensland, Australia.

Tracee was a former TAFE teacher and beautician who was relatively successful in business and astute when it came to money matters. This all changed however the day a man called Robert Sigfrid contacted her through the dating site "Are You Interested?" in 2012. Sigfrid claimed to be a US marine on deployment in Afghanistan. They both appeared to have much in common and it wasn't long before Tracee was smitten by her new admirer, and they started to phone each other on a regular basis.

Claiming to have a fortune in gold, Robert Sigfrid convinced Tracee that this would be their future nest egg, but for now he was short of money…. and that's when he starting asking Tracee for financial assistance. Months into the "relationship" they were engaged. Although she had never actually met her fiancée, she felt an obligation to help the man she had fallen in love with. As the pleas for money kept coming Tracee eventually parted with around $100,000.

As Tracee's suspicions grew and she refused to send any more money, Sigfrid eventually revealed himself as a 22 year-old Nigerian who then tried to encourage her to help him scam other unsuspecting victims. He had of course used the stolen photos of a US serviceman with the surname of Sigfrid which he had used to create one of many fake online profiles.

In the months that followed Tracee eventually gathered enough information on her scammer to report him to the military police, though she holds little hope of recovering any money she lost, and can only hope for an eventual conviction as the investigation is still on-going as far as we know. There is a much more detailed account of Tracee's story in "The Sydney Morning Herald."

In the time that has passed since her experience with being scammed, Tracee has led a crusade to fight romance scammers and has featured in several TV interviews and newspaper articles in her native Australia. She also heads up an established Facebook Anti-Romance scam group (TFB) together with her admin team, to offer support and advice to scam victims and those who are unsure about their "online relationships". Indeed, the knowledge Tracee has gained through experience and research has undoubtedly saved several women from the same fate that she had to endure herself.

We asked Tracee to complete a questionnaire comprising of ten questions that we felt were relevant to the subject of online romance scams, and her responses should be noted by anyone wishing to know more about romance scammers, their techniques, and their "Tricks of the trade." It could save you from the same fate....

1: What first attracted you to your scammer?

I was first attracted to my scammer by the photo he posted of himself on a dating site called 'Are you Interested'. As I have a weakness for men in uniform, in particular military, the attraction was instant. He was well built, with a strong handsome face and amazingly kind looking eyes! Everything I could of hoped for in a man physically, and what was even more attractive is that his profile stated US/Australian dual citizenship'. I was besotted! A wave of lust came over me instantly.

2: What name was he using?

He used the name Robert Sigfrid, a name I have come to learn that many scammers use in conjunction with the photos he was using.

3: How quickly did he declare his love for you?

Love was not a word used for quite some time, as we spent a lot of time on our own private FB page getting to know each other, our hopes, dreams, goals in life. Of course we discussed that after lengthy conversations. We both believed we had met our last love! It was not until he called me approx two months into grooming me that he told me he had fallen in love with me and the feeling was mutual. He was exceptionally good at what he did and seemed to have all the dreams and hopes I had wished for in my life. However, we did debate many topics and we both came to a compromise on where we wanted to live and work.... in Australia and abroad, which in turn, made the whole ordeal seem so much easier to believe, hence, why I say he was very good! Most scammers just agree with whatever you say. Mine did not which I found refreshing and endearing.

4: How long was it before you started to develop any feelings for your scammer?

My physical feelings for my scammer were there straight away! How could they not be when he was all I desired in a man. I was in lust over his photo and many more that he sent me. Love came a bit later and as time passed and we grew to know each other quite well! His interest in my sick mother and my adult children was really nice and I actually believed he cared very much about them, especially after talking to them on the phone. I guess that's when love entered the equation for me! The grooming process was done with absolute perfection. He now had me head over heels in love.

5: What was his occupation...or what did he claim to be?

He was a US Marine when I met him, posted to Afghanistan on his 2nd deployment and had served time in our ADF (Australian Defence Force) straight out of school for three years, and then he moved back to the USA to his parents (fathers home) in Florida, to try to get into the US army which he did, and he made it his life career.

6: Roughly how long was it before he asked you for financial assistance?

He took a few months to ask for financial assistance as he prided himself on looking after me and my mother! Just another sneaky way of tricking me into thinking he was genuine and real. Then came the crunch.... he could not access his military funds due to problems accessing bank accounts because of a breakdown in electronics, so he asked me to send him approx $780 US to pay fees on a bank vault in Kabul. That's where it all started until I was eventually bled dry! I did ask for the original vault invoice which he sent but it was a damn good forgery and I called the phone number on the invoice, and could not understand a word they said! So I believed him pretty much the whole way through. I was so in love, and so blinded by his lies that I just kept sending him money whenever he requested it.

7: How long was it before you began to suspect that you were corresponding with a scammer?

My suspicions arose when he started asking me for more money to feed his troops. The bank vault fees were more believable though at this point I started to doubt the whole thing. The request though for money for food for soldiers under his command hit me like a ton of bricks! I knew then something was not right and questioned this demand. He then became very angry as I refused to send another dime (which would have been borrowed money). Then followed the abusive threats, death threats, and discovering the unauthorized use of my internet photos. I refused to budge though, calling him a liar as I no longer believed a word he said. Eventually he confessed he was a scammer, detailing all he said and did to me and my family in order to steal as much money as he possibly could from me. Then I went downhill into the deepest darkest depths of depression! I thought I would never get over it. But, I was lucky to be saved by a dear friend who taught me to fight back!

8: Did he get angry when you started to question his identity?

Angry is not a strong enough word! He was beside himself with rage, anger, hate, and revenge as his money train had hit a dead end. Some nights in the middle of the night he would ring and tell me there was a gang of men coming to my house if I did not send more money. They would rape and murder my mother and make me watch. Then they would do the same to me. Yes, I was scared at first but not for long! I called their bluff and told them we were waiting with our AFP, the local police and were armed and ready! (all lies) but it worked. Then the threats stopped! He could not get another cent out of me so his threats were pointless.

9: What were your financial losses during your association with your scammer?

My total losses to my scammer were just over $100,000 Australian dollars which was all of my money and additional money I had borrowed. I have receipts for approx. $87,000…. however my house was flooded (2011/2012 / 2012-2013, two years running) during the duration of my scam and I lost some very important documentation pertaining to the scam and of course, personal documents too. I will never see that money again…..

10: Is there any advice you would like to offer to others who may be inclined to fall for a romance scam?

Well I think you need to avoid being drawn in by images and love at first sight. Once you are smitten by a profile photo then it's that much easier to be manipulated by the person behind it. Scammers will almost always use attractive photos stolen from legitimate profiles, and of course are usually well versed in scamming techniques and the characters they have created. Forget how nice they look and watch out for any signs that might suggest that the person you are talking to could be a fake.

Consistent poor use of grammar is a giveaway, especially if they claim to come from the USA, UK, or Australia. The overuse of romantic verses and poetry is another. Declarations of love a short time into your acquaintance should also raise alarm bells. As flattering as it may be, the clincher is when they ask for money. Your scammer may have adopted one of the following careers in an effort to impress….. a senior ranking military man, an architect, a construction contractor, a banker, ship Captain, or one of many other well heeled occupations, but somehow they always seem to have financial problems. In less than a month they will often ask you to help them out of a tight spot by sending them a few hundred dollars because they are temporarily short of money and they will pay you back at a later date. If you agree and send money then they will soon ask you for more, and the deeper you get drawn into the scam, the more you stand to lose.

If you're new online lover seems too good to be true, then he probably is. Don't ever send money to someone you have never met. You'll never get it back when the penny finally drops that you have been scammed.

Interview by Stephen Lee Ostrowski

USEFUL WEBSITES

http://www.romancescam.com

http://www.male-scammers.com

http://www.romancescams.org

http://www.actionfraud.police.uk

http://www.datingnmore.com/fraud/scam_database.html

https://www.scamwarners.com

http://romancescamsnow.com

http://www.cid.army.mil/romancescam.html

http://scamdigger.com/gallery

http://www.419eater.com

https://en.wikipedia.org/wiki/Romance_scam

https://www.scamwatch.gov.au/types-of-scams/dating-romance

http://ghana.usembassy.gov/romance_scam.html

http://www.russian-dating-scams.com/scams/first_things_to_know.htm

http://www.scammers.ru

The following titles by Stephen Lee Ostrowski are available on Amazon.com in paperback or Kindle

"Hello My New Best friend" (The Russian Girlfriend Scams)

IT STARTS WITH THE CLICK OF A MOUSE

STEPHEN LEE OSTROWSKI

GERTY BITES BACK

FACEBOOK FAKES

STEPHEN LEE OSTROWSKI

GERTY BITES AGAIN

FACEBOOK FAKES

STEPHEN LEE OSTROWSKI

Broken

*Written by Judi Huggins
and
Stephen Lee Ostrowski*

Research by Judi Huggins

Edited for publication by Stephen Lee Ostrowski

<u>Disclaimer:</u>

Made in the USA
Coppell, TX
31 May 2022

78331043R00070